THE PRESIDENT AS EDUCATOR

Scholars Press

Studies in Theological Education

Christian Identity and Theological Education   Joseph C. Hough, Jr./
John B. Cobb, Jr.

Vision and Discernment: Charles M. Wood
An Orientation in Theological Study

The Arts in Theological Education: Wilson Yates
New Possibilities for Integration

Beyond Clericalism: Joseph C. Hough, Jr./
The Congregation as a Focus for Theological   Barbara G. Wheeler
Education

The Education of the Practical Theologian: Don S. Browning/
Responses to Joseph Hough and John Cobb's   David Polk/
Christian Identity and Theological Education   Ian S. Evison

Piety and Intellect: The Aims and Purposes   Glenn T. Miller
of Ante-Bellum Theological Education

Religious Studies, Theological Studies
and the University-Divinity School   Joseph Mitsuo Kitagawa

The President as Educator:
A Study of the Seminary Presidency   Neely Dixon McCarter

THE PRESIDENT AS EDUCATOR
A Study of the Seminary Presidency

by
Neely Dixon McCarter

Scholars Press
Atlanta, Georgia

THE PRESIDENT AS EDUCATOR
A Study of the Seminary Presidency

by
Neely Dixon McCarter

© 1996
Scholars Press

Library of Congress Cataloging in Publication Data
McCarter, Neely Dixon, 1929–
 The president as educator : a study of the seminary presidency /
by Neely Dixon McCarter.
  p.   cm. — (Scholars Press studies in theological education)
 Includes bibliographical references (p.   ).
 ISBN 0-7885-0210-7 (alk. paper)
 1. Theological seminary presidents—United States.   I. Title.
II. Series.
BV4166.5.M37   1996
207'.73'0922—dc20   95-26369
                                               CIP

Printed in the United States of America
on acid-free paper

dedicated to

FRED R. STAIR
President Emeritus of
Union Theological Seminary in Virginia

friend, mentor, colleague

who transformed significant dimensions of an institution
with such grace, skill, and humility that it
was hardly noticed

TABLE OF CONTENTS

PREFACE

Several years ago Dr. Craig Dykstra came to Pacific School of Religion to deliver the E. T. Earl Lectures. I was president of the school at the time. During his stay in Berkeley we had occasions to discuss what we considered to be needs in the world of theological education. One of the concerns that I had had for some years related to the presidency of seminaries. While much research had been done about various aspects of the theological enterprise, very little of that work focused on presidents.

The possibility of such a study had been turning over in my mind for years. For more than two decades I worked with presidents of many types of institutions on the committees of the Association of Theological Schools (ATS). During my twelve years at Pacific School of Religion I was part of the Graduate Theological Union, a consortium of ten institutions; this provided me with extensive opportunities to observe and work with presidents from different traditions. I also had numerous conversations with presidents throughout the country in gatherings called by foundations, as I served on accrediting teams for the ATS and regional associations, and as a consultant to other schools. I not only developed many significant friendships among the colleagues with whom I worked, but also felt and experienced along with them the problems and successes, the joys and pain of the office of president.

Craig Dykstra shared my concern for the presidents of theological schools. After a number of consultations with a variety of people, including the staff at the Lilly Endowment, I submitted a proposal for a Planning Grant through the Graduate Theological Union of Berkeley. After a year (1991-92) of further exploration and research, a request was made for a major grant for a study of the presidency.

Beginning in the summer of 1992, the project got underway. Approximately eighty persons were involved, many of them presidents or retired presidents. Taking part in the project were an oral historian, Virginia Geddes; a sociologist of religion, Wade Clark Roof; church historians Erskine Clarke, Robert Wister, and Joseph White; and Marian Gade, a specialist in the field of the administration of higher education. Mark Holman, then a Ph.D. student at the University of California, Berkeley, handled research on the calling of presidents and has published a booklet dealing with that subject titled, *Presidential Search in Theological Schools: Process Makes a Difference.*[1]

The presidents who wrote memoirs, those who met in groups to discuss the issues, and those who were interviewed by me or others, will go unnamed for the most part. They wrote and spoke confidentially in a very personal and honest fashion and it seems wise not to attach their names to specific references or quotations. From time to time a name does appear in the text, but only with permission of the president involved. My original intention was to have numerous quotations from these presidents in the printed text. I found, however, that this made the book too long and settled for using the insights gained from the presidents, with only a few direct quotes. In many ways this volume is the product of the fellowship of leaders in the Association of Theological Schools.

The research was spread over a three-year period, and, as previously noted, some publications have already been issued; others will be forthcoming. Underlying the entire project is the hope that the enterprise of theological education will be strengthened as we understand more adequately this aspect of the governance of these institutions.

During the past three years I have been fortunate to have an advisory committee that has met twice a year to help assess ideas, evaluate documents, and make helpful suggestions for enhancing the study. I am indebted to Leander Keck, Professor and former Dean of Yale Divinity School; Samuel Spencer, President Emeritus of Davidson College; Timothy Lull, Dean of the Pacific Lutheran Theological School; Douglas Sloan, Professor of History and Education at Teacher's College, Columbia University; William Baumgaertner, former Rector of Saint Paul Seminary School of Divinity and Associate Director of the ATS; and Robert Lynn, former Senior Executive Vice President of the Lilly Endowment. Bob Lynn has been a friend as well as a major contributor to my thinking ever since I was a graduate student; he has continued in that role with this project.

Good counsel also was received from Fred Hofheinz, Program Director, Religion, the Lilly Endowment, as well as from Leon Pacala, formerly Executive Director of the ATS, and James Waits, the current Director. Barbara Wheeler, President of Auburn Seminary, has served as friend and wise counselor for many years. I continue to be in her debt as she devoted many hours to reading and discussing with me the content of this book. Sara Little, Professor Emeritus of Christian Education, Union Theological Seminary in Virginia, read the manuscript and shared her wisdom in a most helpful manner. Judy Dodd, formerly of Pacific School of Religion, carefully corrected the manuscript, improved the style, and in general strengthened the material. The good people in the offices of the Graduate Theological Union, especially the Business Office, also have been exceptionally helpful throughout.

Inherent in what I have said is the debt all of us in theological education owe to the Lilly Endowment for supporting and encouraging not only scholarship and research but also programmatic training and education for participants in the theological community. The work of the Lilly Endowment has significantly affected this aspect of religious life in North America. Certainly the health, strength, and hope found in many theological institutions is due in no small part to the persons and resources of this remarkable foundation.

Neely Dixon McCarter
Dillon Beach, California
March 13, 1995

NOTES

[1] This booklet is available through the Association of Theological Schools, 10 Summit Park Drive, Pittsburgh, PA 15275-1103.

1

THE PUZZLE

I watched a videotape some months ago of the very moving retirement party honoring David A. Hubbard who served as president of Fuller Theological Seminary for thirty years. Distinguished business executives, recognized scholars, members of the Fuller administrative staff, and leaders from the theological enterprise gave testimonies to the years of shared leadership that not only made Fuller into a major theological center but also contributed to the shaping of the evangelical movement in the last half of the twentieth century. The occasion was one of warmth, genuine affection, and profound appreciation for a person and his work. The institution, the faith community, and the person celebrated three decades of growth, struggle, and joy.

Not long before watching that tape I had lunch with a person who recently had left the presidency of a seminary. His tenure was a relatively brief one. He too spoke with passion and feeling, but his were words of the hurt he had experienced, of the bitterness of being rejected as an "outsider" whose ideas were pushed aside without thoughtful consideration, of the dread of faculty meetings which he found depressing. He was convinced the trustees had not told him the truth about the situation, if they had even known it themselves. He never found a niche—his place, his role—in the life of the institution. He now sees himself as a liberated man out from under an intolerable burden.

Both stories can be multiplied. The presidency of a theological institution is a source of joy to some and a cause of incredible pain for others. It is a long and happy ministry for some and a bitter, brief experience for others. Even if we assume there are many presidencies that fall between these two extremes, the nature of the office is still puzzling. It is perplexing when search committees looking for candidates for the position often report

1

they cannot find an acceptable person. Many searches flounder and must start over before successfully locating an appropriate candidate. On the other hand, one hears people—some pastors and some academics—who vow that if they could only become president of a seminary, they could alter the way theological education is envisioned and consequently change the future shape of the church. To them, the job looks exciting and challenging, overflowing with possibilities as well as prestige and many rewards. So on the one hand, we have empty-handed search committees, and on the other hand we have rooms full of aspiring volunteers!

There is something baffling about this situation. What is going on? Does the presidency hold joy and meaning for the occupants, or is it so difficult that persons are crushed by it? Is it all a matter of finding the right person for the right job? Is it unrealistic to imagine bringing about change in these institutions? If one were to do so, would the life of the church be appreciably affected? Why is it that some individuals decline offers to consider the position while others line up to accept them?

A recent magazine carried stories of the sudden departure of two presidents. Why is the tenure of presidents getting shorter and shorter? What can presidents realistically expect to do with their energies and talents when they accept the office? These and other matters need to be explored.

It is almost commonplace these days to begin a book by suggesting there is a crisis in the area addressed by the writer. While many declare this is the case with the presidency of seminaries, I believe that language may be a bit strong. I do believe, however, there are reasons for serious concern. I have alluded to a few of these. It is true, for example, that seminary presidents do not ordinarily have the long tenures once fairly common. It can be argued that short terms, especially three to five years, do not provide stable leadership or allow a president time to exert an appreciable amount of influence. At the same time, the fact that some people do not linger long in the office might be a good thing; they may do infinite harm if they do not "fit." I hope our investigation will cast light on reasons for these shorter presidential terms.

Another area of concern involves search committee frustration with an apparent shortage of viable candidates. The fact that many institutions are limited in their searches to persons from a particular tradition, denomination, or religious order, makes part of this problem understandable; but other issues must be involved. Are the parameters of the job understood? What do presidents actually do with their time and what kinds of influence can they realistically expect to exercise? Could this lack of clarity impede the search process by discouraging candidates? Does the confusion about the nature of the job contribute to the paucity of strong candidates and compound the work of search committees?

Multiple notions about the presidential job float around in churches and the academy. One notion is that the president of any institution in our time is obliged to raise funds; this type of activity is distasteful to many people, especially academics and clergy, from whose ranks presidents usually come. Related to this is the impression that such positions involve a heavy investment in administration, another activity that tends to daunt persons in the presidential pool. Administration is not ordinarily looked upon as a "worthy calling" in clerical and academic circles. Is this an appropriate characterization of the job? One way or the other, how should administration be understood in theological institutions?

Another image of the seminary president is that of the "embattled" manager. The president is seen as a person trying to run an institution under fire from the churches for failing to prepare persons to do what churches want them to do, while fighting with faculty who would rather do research or travel than teach. Or, the president is caught in the crossfire between trustees demanding a reduction in the budget and faculty and staff desiring to expand their numbers or increase their salaries. Is the president's role best envisioned as a "manager?"

How can a person caught in such conflicting expectations exercise leadership? In addition, educational institutions are famous for "shared governance," dividing the decision-making process among several bodies; this appears to leave the president responsible for everything, but having little or no power to make effective decisions. Presidents have written about their frustration with these matters and researchers have documented the problems. How does one view educational leadership in these types of institutions? Can a president actually lead as expected to by trustees and other constituencies, including faculty and students?

These are serious questions, stated here in exaggerated form. But they are questions that presidents themselves reflect on from time to time, questions that candidates and governing boards ask themselves. Such questions do not necessarily constitute a crisis, but they do raise matters that need investigating; they invite proposals as to how we might respond.

After years of reflection on the seminary presidency, Leon Pacala, who served as president of a seminary and later as executive for the Association of Theological Schools, states:

> The profession as a whole suffers from the absence of clear conceptualization of the defining nature and primary roles of presidential leadership.[1]

To define the nature and primary roles of the president and to offer a clear conceptualization of the office is the purpose of this book. In dealing with these matters I shall draw upon the experience of current and past presidents of theological institutions, thereby keeping this document rooted in reality and in touch with the concrete matters that compose the life and work of presidents. On the other hand, I do want to present a thesis, make a case for a particular point of view, if you please. It is my contention that the president of a theological school should be understood primarily as an educator. I do not think this is simply a matter of taste or preference, but is inherent in the understanding of education, especially in light of the recognition of the teacher or educator/teacher in the Christian tradition. While a president engages in a multitude of tasks, including administration, management, and fundraising, these latter activities do not lie at the core of that which enables a president to discover the unity in his or her own work or the purpose of the institution served. While I shall argue that envisioning the president as educator can empower the person to function with integrity in the office, I will not pretend that this solves the many problems facing presidents of theological schools in our time. But I do believe it is a conceptualization of the office that has merit for presidents and their constituencies.

Before stating my position, I will examine some of the changes that have taken place in the office since the founding of the first seminary in 1808. These vignettes will help us understand how the office has been affected by the ecclesiastical traditions of the schools, by the society in which the institutions exist, and by the personalities of the persons who have occupied the office (Chapter 2). Having noted the forces that create the duties and possibilities of the office, we shall describe what people occupying the position today actually do. We will note how much of this activity appears to be something other than education (Chapter 3). We then shall see why it is appropriate to call the president an educator and how the many duties of the presidency can be understood as essential to the educational process and as practices deeply rooted in the Christian tradition (Chapter 4).

Next, we will interpret educational leadership and administration, relating them to the shared governance found in most educational institutions and to the notion of the president as educator (Chapter 5). Regardless of what understanding of the office one may have, there are personal dimensions of the job—such as the call to the task, the support of the president, and the appropriate time to exit the office—that need to be considered (Chapter 6). None of the foregoing matters can eliminate the systemic problems which make the presidency difficult and demanding (Chapter 7). Finally, we will look at how the conception of the presidency found in this volume can help persons think about the institution they know best and I will offer some straws in the wind about the future. Like certain other positions in our time, the presidency of theological seminaries is a challenging one because it is crucially important for the life of the church in the years ahead (Chapter 8).

THE ENTERPRISE

Let us be clear about the enterprise we are discussing. Not many people know a great deal about theological institutions, let alone their presidents. Yet a very thoughtful student and leader of institutions in the United States, the late Robert K. Greenleaf, once suggested there was no institution in our society that had greater potential for constructive influence on the whole of our society than the theological school.[2] Anyone who would read this book is probably inclined to agree that theological schools are of primary importance to the church and the world.

Nevertheless, we need to call attention to the fact that the theological enterprise is a small operation compared to many others, even within the arena of higher education. The institutions studied as part of this project were the schools accredited by the Association of Theological Schools in the United States and Canada. This includes some 226 schools that are either accredited or applying for accreditation with ATS in 1994.[3] Assuming each has a president, we are dealing with little more than two hundred people and positions. By contrast, one can note that there are approximately 4,000 institutions of higher education in the United States and Canada. There are 345 colleges and universities in the state of California alone.

In addition, seminaries are very small institutions; the total enrollment of all of the schools in the fall of 1993 was 63,618. That is counting everyone who takes a class! If one counts "full time equivalent" or FTE (the total number of students divided by the number of courses that constitute a "full class load"), there were only 48,236. By comparison, Ohio State University has more than 58,500 students on its main campus! The

University of Texas has some 49,000. Most of these 226 ATS schools have 150 students (FTE) or less. Seventy-nine schools have between 150 and 300 students while only four schools have more than 1,000. The largest school has about 2,600 students. Clearly, we are talking about small institutions.[4]

While I acknowledge that we are dealing with a small group of institutions and persons in our society, their significance for the future of the churches and our common life means that we are dealing with an important minority.

DEFINING TERMS

Before proceeding, I will define some of the terms I will be using. By now a number of readers are no doubt agitated by my constant use of the term *president* or *presidency* in light of their use of cognates from their own traditions: *rector* or *dean* or *principal*. *Dean*, for example, is used by divinity schools located within a university and by Episcopalians to refer to the leader of one of their seminaries. The head of a Canadian theological institution is usually referred to as *principal*. Roman Catholics have for centuries called the heads of their seminaries *rectors*. Some persons writing about theological education prefer the term *CEO* or Chief Executive Officer, an expression that, though meaningful to many in our society, offends an equal number of persons in the academic community. There now exists within the ATS a number of combinations of the preceding: rector/president or president/dean. I shall use the word *president* to refer to the chief executive officer; it is the term most frequently used and is understood by persons engaged in various forms of higher education. I will from time to time use the other terms such as dean or rector or CEO; but for the most part, I will refer to the president and presidency.

I have struggled with the use of inclusive language and have rewritten many sentences to avoid using the personal pronoun, but this cannot always be done. I am also aware that several traditions which are a part of the ATS do not allow for ordination of women and therefore would not have women as presidents of schools for the education of clergy. Nevertheless, in instances when a personal pronoun is necessary, I have chosen to alternately use the feminine and masculine with reference to faculty members as well as presidents and trust this language will not be offensive to any group.

In addition, it should be noted that institutions devoted to the education of clergy bear a variety of names: university divinity school, school of theology, theological seminary, school of ministry, school of religion. For the purpose of our discussion, I shall refer to all of these as seminaries and theological schools. I will use such terms as schools, institutions, and seminaries for the sake of variety.

The denominational affiliation of a school and/or a university is yet another designation. Some theological schools are part of monasteries, are operated by religious orders, or are independent of both universities and denominations. Denominations or universities may own and control certain of these schools, though the degree of control may vary greatly. As we move into this study we will see that these variations along with others contribute to the shaping of many unique institutions.[4]

The expression *theological education* can refer simply to the education of Christians; they receive a theological education at home and/or in the church school, meaning they are educated in the beliefs and practices of the tradition. But it can also refer to the educational process that takes place in seminaries. Students are exposed to a learning experience that is called a theological education; it consists of courses as well as the formative influence of the school's ethos. This book is concerned with the role of the president in the educational processes of theological schools.

The use of the phrase *seminary presidency* implies a particular office that can be described and found in each theological school. While commonality exists, the uniqueness of each school makes the office referred to by the term *presidency* different in some respects in each institution. There is really no such thing as *the* seminary presidency.[5]

RELATION OF OTHER LITERATURE

In recent years there has been a proliferation of literature concerning theological education. David Kelsey suggests that

> ...the central question in the recent debate has been this:"What is the nature and purpose of specifically *theological* education? What sets it off from other apparently closely related academic enterprises as, precisely, *theological* education?"[6]

The extraordinary significance of this discussion cannot be overestimated.[7] It is vital for theological institutions—whether located in a university or freestanding, whether denominational or independent—that faculty members, administrators, and trustees carry on this dialogue and debate. This has to do with the *calling* of the institution, with its *vocation*. It is of primary concern that an institution formulate a purpose which permeates the entire establishment; it has to do with who is called to teach, the way the teaching interaction is conceived, and the structure of the common life.

This book will borrow from the ongoing discussion about theological education, particularly that of Professor Kelsey; however, it does not intend to be a part of that discussion. This book will focus on the office of the president in a school's life and operation. While the president *alone* does not set the purpose of the institution, she is an active participant in the continuing process that determines, reviews, and renews that purpose. Moreover, the president is responsible for seeing that the resources, curricular designs, staffing, and general shape of the institution are such that its purpose is carried out with integrity. It is this role of the president that concerns us here.

There is another genre of literature dealing with the ways presidents should be called, how they should be evaluated, how they should delegate and organize. All of these are worthy matters, for there are many "how to" questions that face presidents every day. How to manage effectively, how to develop plans for the future, how to strengthen a board, how to find trustees. These are important issues. There may even be some help for those questions in this book, but our task in this volume is to examine critically the understanding of the presidency as a dimension of the life of a theological institution. My hope is that the book will engender a more adequate nurturing of the office of the president, thereby invigorating and strengthening theological institutions in their larger task of nurturing God's people.

There is yet another body of literature that deals with college and university presidencies including research related to the administration of higher education. Since there are many parallels between the presidency of a small college and those of theological schools, I will refer to germane portions of this material.

AUDIENCES

Who might profit from reading this volume? First, and perhaps foremost, are trustees. It has been said the most important duty of trustees is to call an able person to the presidency of their school. Someone else proposed that the most significant responsibility of the trustees is to support the president and make the work more attractive. I hope this book will contribute to fulfilling both of these tasks more adequately.

Second, there is always a group of new presidents in theological schools. The Association of Theological Schools attempts to help orient these people to their new lives. Perhaps this volume also will help. Third, there are a number of folks out there—in parishes, serving as deans or academic vice presidents of colleges or seminaries, church judicatory leaders, and others—who might consider becoming a president were they invited to do so. I hope in this volume they can learn something about the position and the possibilities.

Fourth, all of the people involved in the enterprise of theological education could profit from a clearer grasp of the president's role and relationship to the rest of the community. As Robert Lynn, a veteran observer and participant in the enterprise suggests, the *faculty* in particular need to rethink their stance toward the position and what it means for the life of the institution.[8] So it is hoped that trustees, staff, faculty, and students will find this work useful, especially as it relates to governance.

SOURCES

Some of the sources used in writing this study have already been mentioned. However, the major contribution was made by research done as part of the project, "The Study of the Seminary Presidency," funded by Lilly Endowment, Inc. and described briefly in the Preface. Data was generated, first, by interviews with dozens of presidents and persons involved in theological education; second, by approximately twenty-five presidents who wrote memoirs, or their reflections on their experience in the office. Third, ten former presidents were interviewed as part of an oral history component of the study. Fourth, several persons did historical studies of the rise and development of the office since 1808. Fifth, there was a sociological study of the perception of the office by leaders of selected denominations. Sixth, there was a study of the search process for new presidents.

Finally, I bring to this study my own experience as dean, president, trustee, and consultant; I also have read widely about the office of the president in the field of higher education, have interviewed a great many individuals, and have participated in dialogue with a number of groups while gathering material for this writing. Many, therefore, have contributed to the information found here, though I assume responsibility for the way in which it is interpreted and used.

NOTES

[1] Leon Pacala, "The Presidential Experience in Theological Education: A Study of Executive Leadership," *Theological Education*, vol. xxix, no.1 (Autumn 1992), 32.

[2] Robert K.Greenleaf, *Seminary As Servant*(The Center for Applied Studies, Peterborough, N.H., 1983 edition), 8.

[3] Gail Buchwalter King, Editor,*Fact Book on Theological Education* (Pittsburgh: The Association of Theological Schools, 1994), i. The figures used in this section are taken from the 1993-1994 *Fact Book,* which contains information supplied to the ATS by member schools in the fall of 1993. These are the latest figures available. The figure of 226 schools for 1994 is found in the introduction to the *Fact Book,* but 219, representing the member schools in the fall of 1993, is used throughout the 1993-1994 book.

[4] Ibid., 23-93, the section on enrollment.

[5] One final matter with reference to terminology. Occasionally in the writing, you will find references to particular types of schools; terms like "mainline denominational" or "evangelical independent" will be used. These expressions most often appear in sections of the writing that are based on research, work done either by participants in this particular project or by others, particularly the Auburn Seminary Center for the Study of Theological Education and the Association of Theological Schools. President Barbara Wheeler of Auburn Seminary explained the grouping of schools as follows:

> The system of classifying schools used here was developed by the Hartford Center and Auburn Seminary; institutions are divided first by whether or not they have a formal relationship to a religious body, then by religious tradition. In general, denominational schools whose sponsoring denominations belong to the National Council of Churches are classified as "mainline," although a few such schools that have emphasized their evangelical identity have been classified as evangelical. Independent Protestant institutions are classified by their public identity as mainline or evangelical.

Barbara Wheeler, "Chief Executives of Theological Schools: A Profile", December, 1992, a report developed for this project by Auburn Seminary, 2.

[6] David H. Kelsey, *Between Athens and Berlin: The Theological Education Debate* (Grand Rapids: Eerdmans, 1993), 2.

[7] While these are not the only contributors to the ongoing dialogue, they represent some of the key players. Edward Farley, *Theologia: The Fragmentation and Unity of Theological Education* (Philadelphia: Fortress Press, 1983) and *The Fragility of Knowledge: Theological Education in the Church and the University* (Philadelphia: Fortress Press, 1988). David H. Kelsey, *To Understand God Truly: What's Theological About a Theological School* (Louisville: Westminster/John Knox Press, 1992) and *Between Athens and Berlin: The Theological Education Debate* (Grand Rapids: Eerdmans, 1993). Joseph C.Hough, Jr. and Barbara G. Wheeler,editors, *Beyond Clericalism: The Congregation as a Focus for Theological Education,* (Atlanta: Scholars Press,1988). Joseph C. Hough,Jr. and John B. Cobb,Jr.,*Christian Identity and Theological Education* (Chico, CA.: Scholars Press, 1985). Max L. Stackhouse, *Apologia: Contextualization, Globalization, and Mission in Theological Education* (Grand Rapids: Eerdmans, 1988).Barbara G. Wheeler and Edward Farley, editors, *Shifting Boundaries:Contextual Approaches to the Structure of Theological Education* (Louisville: Westminster/John Knox Press, 1991). Charles M. Wood, *Vision and Discernment* (Atlanta:

Scholars Press, 1985). Joseph Mitsuo Kitagawa, editor, *Religious Studies, Theological Studies and the University-Divinity School* (Atlanta: Scholars Press, 1992). Richard John Neuhaus, editor, *Theological Education and Moral Formation* (Grand Rapids: Eerdmans, 1992).

[8] Robert W. Lynn, "Coming Over the Horizon" in *Good Stewardship*, edited by Barbara Taylor and Malcolm Warford (Washington: The Association of Governing Boards, 1991), 55.

2

AN EVER-CHANGING OFFICE

Our purpose in this chapter is to look briefly at some specific changes which have occurred in the presidency since the founding of theological schools in the United States. Certain situations have been selected while others have been omitted. The diverse institutions that compose the theological education enterprise make the task of selection hazardous; one is bound to neglect significant events that affected certain seminaries. In addition, an adequate history of the presidency would need to record the interplay of the ecclesial traditions of the institutions, the ethos of particular schools, the personality of persons occupying the position at any given time, as well as the sociocultural context.[1] This brief presentation, on the other hand, identifies a few of the changes that contributed to making the presidency what it is today.

THE SCHOLAR-PASTOR

Clergy were being prepared for their calling long before there were seminaries in North America. Young men (and they were all men in those days) "read theology" with the president of the college from which they had just graduated or with a prominent pastor who had a reasonably good library. Various forms of apprenticeship were developed to enable churches in the new world to have pastors without sending to England, Scotland, France, or Germany, though this was an accepted practice for decades. Other groups did not worry about education; the "calling of God" was sufficient preparation for ministry. For still others, a college education was considered adequate.

The founding of Andover Seminary in 1808 is generally accepted as the beginning of theological schools as we know them.[2] Following the lead of this institution, dozens of such schools were created in a very few years and their number continued to grow until the Civil War. For a number of reasons, most of these schools operated with a board of trustees rather than directly under the authority of a denomination.

The Roman Catholics attempted to follow the guidelines set for the training of clergy by the sixteenth-century Council of Trent. Accordingly, such education was under the supervision of bishops in their own locations. As bishops appeared on the American scene, they began establishing schools for the education of priests, such as Bishop John Carroll did in Baltimore in 1791. Other seminaries followed, though more slowly than among the Protestants.

The Roman Catholic seminaries reflected their tradition's organization, with each bishop being something of an island unto himself, possessing incredible power and freedom. He could found and maintain a school for ministry without the need for trustees in the sense of an independent board with final authority. Neither did he need a group to support the school, though in fact he might locate supporters for this and other undertakings.

In neither Protestant nor Catholic schools, however, were there presidents in the sense that we ordinarily use the word today. In Protestant schools, a faculty member, often the senior member of the faculty or the professor of theology, was designated *president*. This usually implied moderating at faculty gatherings and presenting concerns of the faculty to trustees. He was expected to see that the details of the community were handled by himself or another faculty member. The person was assumed to be primarily a scholar and teacher; the position acknowledged his seniority and the need for orderliness in the school's affairs. One might suggest that this person functioned as senior pastor of a loosely organized, local congregation.

In the Roman Catholic schools, rectors were appointed in accordance with canon law. Such a person was to oversee the curriculum as well as the spiritual and pastoral formation of students. On the American scene, however, rectors had to deviate from time to time from the norm set by Trent in order to continue to maintain their seminaries. For example, the rector of Mount St. Mary's in Emmitsburg, a Suplician, had to combine clerical formation with lay education to sustain the seminary, which was very small.[3] Nevertheless, rectors were primarily teachers and pastors.

In some Protestant schools, members of the boards of trustees, the presbytery, or some other local judicatory handled many of the administrative matters such as gathering funds, setting examinations, and providing a meeting place for classes. Trustees were thus integrally related to the seminaries and provided an ideal form of accountability since denominations were not structured to make the schools accountable to them.

In these early theological institutions, whether Roman Catholic or Protestant, the president was a faculty member who carried a few extra duties to facilitate the educational process.

INCREASING TASKS

While in theory the faculty handled the day to day running of these early seminaries, institutional demands had a way of growing. Space had to be found for classes; books procured for the library; arrangements made for meals. Some institutions appointed a person to search for monies— "agents" or "financial agents," as they were frequently called. These agents were not necessarily members of the faculty, though some were. The creation of another position at Union Theological Seminary in Virginia in 1830, "the Intendant," is illustrative of what was happening in schools in general:

> He was the overseer of the practical day-to-day operations of the school...At times, the Intendant was a student or a recent graduate, but more often a faculty member, and occasionally a local member of the Board. The Intendant worried with housing, and building maintenance, student fees, food preparation, garbage disposal, student deportment and (interestingly enough) cattle. As late as 1891, the *Rules* of the seminary prohibits students "throwing out of the windows slops, water, fruitrinds, and parings, or anything whatever..." If students were a problem for the Intendant, so also were the cows. Repeatedly, the Intendant warned that the "grazing of horses or cattle and the hitching or staking of such in the front yard of the Seminary...(is)...positively forbidden." One Intendant posted signs at each entrance to the seminary grounds that began: "All cattle are hereby notified...," on the assumption, apparently, that cows which had been attending the seminary on such a regular basis could, by now, surely read his instructions![4]

The internal operation of the school prompted the office of Intendant while the need to find funds gave rise to the Agent. The internal demands in Roman Catholic schools created the "business manager" or "procurator" while the bishop was responsible for finding the funds necessary for the operation of the school and for adjudicating serious matters.[5] And so the duties assigned to the president began to expand and other "administrators" were added. The president could no longer simply be convener of the faculty.

One can say that from 1808 until the late 1800s there was basically no one occupying a position of "president" as the word is used today, but the increasing duties laid upon the president indicated that changes would soon take place.

THE PERMANENT PRESIDENT

In October of 1900 John Knox McLean, President of Pacific Theological Seminary in Oakland, California, spoke to the Conference of Congregational Seminaries in St. Louis. He titled his address, "The Presidency of Theological Seminaries. Should the Theological Seminary Have A Permanent President; And If So, What Should Be The Powers And Duties Of The Office?"

McLean based his remarks on a survey of college and university presidents. They all agreed that seminaries, if they were to be stable, well-endowed, smooth-running institutions, needed a person who is primarily the president, not merely a faculty member who holds the title. Efficiency of operation and the necessity of finding funds were the basic needs. McLean argued that as splendid as they are, board members do not have the time to attend to the multitude of duties that need to be handled. Nor, said he, can a faculty member easily move into the position. If the latter happens

> ...what will most probably result? That which has under similar circumstances so often resulted; resentment on the part of fellow-professors, corporate friction, personal irritation, all-round discord, and general chaos. He is more than likely to find himself a Joseph among his brethren, his best intentions misconceived and thwarted, left alone, stripped of his garment of distinction, in a pit, and with reason to count himself fortunate if he be not given over to the Ishmaelites or other philistines.[6]

McLean's proposal was to remove administration and fund raising from the faculty and lodge it with someone who could specialize in these areas. McLean did not want to conceive of the president as an educator any longer; he preferred "an executive."

> Our great colleges and universities, from the oldest, Harvard in the East, to the youngest, Stanford in the West, have administrative heads,—men by no means destitute of scholarly attainment, but in whom the executive faculty predominates. "Not primarily scholars and secondarily administrators, but the reverse."...the present-day president is, more than anything else, an executive.[7]

It is significant that McLean turned to colleges and universities in identifying and describing the position. Seminaries historically have followed the lead of their sister institutions in higher education *in matters of administration*. They also have experienced some of the same pressures and demands as colleges and universities, though usually a decade or two later. For example, Laurence Veysey, in his discussion of this early twentieth-century period of the American university, notes that the results of the growth in size, the modifying of goals to include more practical fields, the push by the public to admit more and more students to higher education, the organization of the faculty into departments with heads and budgets were contributory to the development of larger and larger administrative staffs and bureaucratic procedures. He states that "administration" came to connote a state of mind, one characterized by institutional management and organizational planning. Administration and faculty became two different things.[8]

This perception of administration eventually developed in theological schools, with similar consequences for faculty/president relationships. Furthermore, this idea, which suggests that the president is the head of a corporation, continues to affect the presidency to this day.

THE STRONG EXECUTIVE

McLean won his argument; most institutions soon had presidents. However, usually the president and some associate, known as the registrar or president's assistant, managed the entire institution. For the most part, Protestant schools were both small and poor.

The same was true in Roman Catholic seminaries in the sense that the size of the school enabled the rector to continue in his traditional role. In many situations there were orders of sisters or brothers who did the laundry, ran the dining room, and maintained the buildings. Since the priests who taught in the schools did not draw regular salaries, bookkeeping and fund raising were not major problems; the procurator handled the day to day matters.[9] Many financial and administrative concerns were located in the bishop's office. The rector still could be seen as a part of the faculty, as a necessary ingredient in the educational institution. The term *president* would have been inappropriate during the early 1900s in Catholic schools.

Approximately twenty-five years after McLean's proposal, in a study of theological education made in 1924, Robert Kelly noted that seminaries had done very little in developing administrative staffs and functions.[10]

Though short on staff, seminaries were being urged during this period to reflect changes taking place in other sectors of higher education. As early as 1899, William Rainey Harper of the University of Chicago proposed major shifts in theological curriculum which sound like those listed by Veysey .[11] The same is true of both the 1924 study by Kelly and the 1934 study by William A. Brown, Mark A. Mays, and others. They also urged reforms in theological education that would incorporate the latest in psychological and pedagogical research concerning both persons and institutions; room should be made in the curriculum for specialization and electives.[12] Theological schools were encouraged to become more "practical," to give students the necessary skills and training they needed to operate a church in the rapidly growing cities of North America. The pressures upon seminaries were not unlike those upon universities, though theological schools remained very small institutions. University- related divinity schools felt the pressures to conform to these changes more than independent schools; Roman Catholic seminaries were hardly disturbed. [13]

To say the corporate model of efficient, executive leadership entered theological education in the early 1900s, bringing with it the office of the president and, at the same time, to describe seminaries during this period as "mom and pop stores" may seem like a contradiction. The model was present, but most schools did not have large staffs or faculties to organize in bureaucratic fashion. This situation contributed to the emergence of strong presidents. In the universities of the time, it was an era of "giants," presidents who exerted their wills to build powerful institutions. Likewise, in the seminaries, the president who was responsible for almost everything and had few, if any, ecclesiastical or governmental regulations or academic strictures upon his office, could basically run an institution according to his best insights. Also, it was not uncommon for him to be an outstanding member of his denomination or tradition and therefore have a great deal of clout among the constituency, as well as within the seminary community. This was true in part at least because these presidents had to rely on churches for students, financial support, and the calling of the school's graduates. Consequently, presidents tended to be very active within their denomination or tradition. They often held positions of power within the bureaucratic structures of the church and in ecumenical organizations. As in the case of colleges and universities, there were powerful presidents who "put their institution on the map." These presidents were thought of as strong church leaders rather than faculty members. Again, one notes that this change in both the perception and role of the president persists unto today.

In the mid-1950s, when H. Richard Niebuhr, James Gustafson, and Daniel Day Williams did their excellent study of theological education, they called attention to the abuse of power frequently found in theological schools run by strong presidents. They took great exception to relegating faculty to library or curriculum committees while the president made the major decisions that shaped the life of the institution.[14]

While the style of these strong presidents may have been distasteful to the faculty, they were frequently, as noted above, persons of vision both for the church and for education. These presidents may have been "executives," but they were ordinarily persons who enabled their seminaries to find a place in the life of the churches.

Today, when many people in church and the academy think of presidents, they frequently—consciously or unconsciously—think of these "giants" who exercised great power both in the schools and within the ecclesiastical environment to make their institutions strong and productive. The power and prestige of the office would be altered due to subsequent changes, yet the memory of these heroic presidents lingers.

THE PIVOTAL YEARS

Following World War II seminaries experienced changes that greatly altered the administrative demands of the theology school. An influx of students, many of whom were married, bringing with them the GI bill, presented numerous challenges. Many postwar students had not prepared for seminary while in college; special attention therefore had to be given to their lack of background in such subjects as philosophy to supplement their earlier education. Frequently their ecclesiastical backgrounds were more varied. Some Lutheran seminaries had to stop teaching their classes in German! While seminaries were delighted to have these students, their presence made life in these small institutions more complex.

All of these changes demanded more staff members to handle the new situations. A president with one assistant could no longer manage. Business offices had to have someone to process government forms and procure married student housing. A registrar was needed to certify papers for the government as well as keep records for accrediting societies. The maintenance staff grew along with new dormitories and apartments; so did the dining room and even the bookstore. Deans of students began to appear to help students find housing and their spouses find jobs; they frequently handled "field education" and arranged for "supply preaching."

Academic deans—many of whom had done very little administration over the years—suddenly found scheduling of classes to be problematic and assessment of students' previous education time consuming. New faculty had to be found to accommodate the growing numbers. Accrediting procedures called for reports and statistics annually.

One can understand the emergence of administrative staffs within the theological school. The president now had so many duties, both within the school and in the larger supporting community, that he frequently needed an assistant in addition to a secretary. The presidency was changing yet again; he was becoming the supervisor of a staff of administrators.

Internal changes within the institutions and the structures of the denominations, government, and accrediting societies outside converged to encourage the rationalization of the organization. The understanding of administration described by Veysey began to develop in the seminaries and the cleavage between the faculty and the administration evolved, carrying with it the notion that faculty handled the education while the president dealt with the corporation.

Canadian schools were not as caught up in these movements toward a corporate model as were those in the United States. The Canadians operated with a principal, as they had done from earliest times; faculty maintained control over most of the school's operations. In most theological schools there was a senate composed of faculty, church representatives, and persons from other educational institutions. This group exercised oversight of the academic programs; boards of directors frequently handled matters like budgets and personnel policies. Since the state and the churches funded the schools, fund raising was not an issue until more recent times. There was little need for large staffs in these institutions.

The Roman Catholic schools also experienced a great influx of students following World War II. Their churches were expanding; the "immigrant church" from Ireland, Germany, Italy, and Poland had come of age. Children of the immigrants had entered the mainstream of American culture and business. Seminary enrollment was at a peak, with 454 seminaries preparing men for the Catholic priesthood in 1965.

The bishop or superior of the sponsoring religious order still appointed the rector and funds basically came from those two sources. There usually were not boards of trustees who handled the policies of the school; that still resided with the bishop or the order. Faculty continued to be members of the priesthood and the curriculum was fairly uniform throughout, following the patterns of classes ordered by the church. The rector did not have to change his role significantly and the term *president* was never used. Following the Second Vatican Council in 1965, however, great ferment and change would take place.[15]

THE ENTREPRENEUR

The period from the late 1960s to the present involves an intricate interplay of societal, denominational, and seminary factors that ushered in significant changes in the office of the president. Before turning to the seminaries, let us first examine the movements within denominations as they responded to society.

During the late 1960s and early 1970s, many mainline denominations experienced considerable disruption.[16] For many reasons denominational staff curtailed or abandoned many of their prior programmatic functions. In their study of Protestant denominational structures, Craig Dystra and James Hudnut-Beumler describe this phenomenon.

> Decisions [by denominations] were made...in the late 1960's to turn national missions activity over to local groups working with Indians, orphans, alcoholics, pregnant teenagers, and African-American schoolchildren. Especially important were decisions to abandon large-scale national youth ministry programs. To speak in marketing terms, the national churches were divesting themselves of some of their most popular products. Given this process alone, one could expect the appeal to the pocketbooks of church members would begin to diminish.[17]

Giving to the churches did decline, and the ravages of inflation made life in all ecclesiastical institutions very difficult. Seminaries were no exception.

Churches also were experiencing the turmoil of the Civil Rights Movement and the Vietnam War. The role of both the government and the church was a matter for heated debate. Young people in and out of churches were accusing their seniors in higher education and in the church of not taking seriously the values they themselves espoused. There was no small amount of disillusionment with the institutions that were supposed to embody the highest and best values of both church and nation.

During this period there was growth in the "evangelical" wing of the churches. Organizations, publications, large meetings, youth movements, colleges, and seminaries sprang up to appeal and minister to this segment of believers. Their publications, conferences, and networks frequently replaced those previously supplied by the denomination.[18] There was also the phenomenon of the charismatic movement, which attracted people regardless of affiliation, both Protestant and Roman Catholic. In like manner, special interest groups emerged; these too, crossed denominational lines. There were groups concerned with abortion, both for and against. There were others advocating for gays and lesbians in the church and those opposed. Traditional ecclesiastical affiliation was weakened; many left the church. Large megachurches with conservative theological and social attitudes attracted many people. The newer evangelical seminaries drew students from mainline denominations as well as independents.

It was also during the mid-1960s that membership in mainline denominations peaked and the economy began to slow. Giving to denominations began its decline. National staffs had to be reduced; those who remained were left with the task of distributing dwindling resources while also developing regulations to govern and control budgets and activities of related institutions which the denominations could no longer fund or service. These limited activities—developing regulations and controlling budgets—evoke the metaphor of "regulatory agencies."[19]

This era witnessed the joining of several denominations or the reuniting of denominations that once before had been a single church. These mergers not only caused people in the pews to feel their old church was now gone but also disrupted patterns of support for seminaries; it sometimes caused two schools from different segments of the merger to unite. These events, together with many others, prompted Robert Wuthnow to suggest that there has been a major restructuring of American religion since World War II.[20]

But let us now turn directly to a discussion of the "restructuring of seminaries." The first element of restructuring was the "academic revolution" of faculty. *The Advancement of Theological Education,* published in 1957, recorded the dissatisfaction of professors who felt excluded from any consideration in the administration of seminaries. Faculty members everywhere shared this concern; consequently, the American Association of University Professors (AAUP) issued a document dealing with "shared governance" in 1966 which is still used as a basis by faculties for sharing decision making regarding educational policy matters. Faculties everywhere were tired of "one-man rule." Faculty members in seminaries, encouraged by accrediting bodies and professional associations, sought to implement governance patterns that assured them of a piece of the action. As we shall see, the emergence of shared governance has changed the presidency of all institutions of higher education as much as any single factor.

The Niebuhr study had decried the poor state of scholarship in theological schools at mid-century. As a consequence, the Rockefeller Brothers Foundation and other groups funded the education of many promising young people for the purpose of generating scholarly faculty members for seminaries. Some institutions selected future faculty members and sent them off to get Ph.D.s at the expense of the school. Being a seminary faculty member had become a profession for which people prepared themselves. While there always had been some faculty who were educated for that purpose, in earlier times many faculty members were persons who had been successful in the parish and moved into theological education later in their careers.

Academic guilds, the gathering of scholars who work in the same field, became more and more important for seminary faculty. From the founding of Andover there had been efforts by faculty members to generate scholarship and publish. But in this era a new emphasis was given to scholarly publication as a basis for promotion and tenure. Kelsey speculates that even Niebuhr and his colleagues in the mid-1950s could not have imagined the intensity and impact of faculty professionalization.[21] Through guilds of scholars, faculty members receive rewards for scholarly research presented in papers or books. Friendships within the guild are frequently stronger than within one's own faculty. In many cases faculty loyalties are to their guilds, not the institutions in which they teach.

By the mid-1970s there were many scholars who preferred to teach in departments of religion in universities rather than in seminaries. These departments, which had once been viewed as "step-children" to the theological schools, were to become the primary fountains of scholarship and publications.

As academic disciplines became more professionalized, the demands for sophisticated programs in the areas of field education, clinical pastoral education, interns in church and society, studios for Christianity and the arts, and others multiplied. Theological education, for both Protestants and Roman Catholics, was becoming not only complex but also very expensive.

While academic guilds added to the administrative work of the school through demands for sabbatics, tenure, promotion, and policies to govern these matters, ecclesiastical and governmental regulations made the search for a new faculty member more complex. Searches began to involve a great deal more in terms of advertising, following procedures to avoid discrimination, and carrying out affirmative action policies in addition to finding the right fields of specialization. The ATS, whose policies are agreed upon by member schools, added many of these requirements to its accrediting procedures. This single issue of faculty hires provides a glimpse of the emergence of "academic regulatory agencies" and their impact on schools. As Veysey noted with respect to American universities, the professionalization and organization of faculty led to increases in administration.

A second element in the restructuring of theological schools resulted from the declining services of denominational bureaucracies. Denominational seminaries were called upon, or volunteered, to supply part of the "goods" formerly produced by the national boards and agencies which were now dwindling. Seminaries were requested to do the continuing education of clergy, undertake lay education, produce literature and conferences for church groups, expand training for mission work or youth ministry, prepare pastors to operate programs for the aging, provide training to use new media, work within the inner city, and any number of other things. All of this was to be done despite inflation that was sapping the resources of theological schools.

Seminaries were not just helping the churches, however; they were also seeking students. Shrinking markets for graduates, declines in church giving, and, in some cases, declining numbers of students seeking the basic ordination degree, encouraged a broadening of purposes for institutions. School administrations and faculties became entrepreneurs seeking new programs, markets, and students. Some within the theological community have spoken of this as "functional sprawl." Old purposes were not so much abandoned as new ones were tacked on. One small institution known to the writer had so many different programs that each member of the faculty headed at least one, and in some cases two, separate programs.

A third element that has forced changes in theological schools is the establishment of local, state, and federal government regulatory agencies as well as standards for accreditation.   As government requirements on accounting procedures came into play in the life of these small institutions, so did IRS regulations about recording gifts; auditing firms were hired and bookkeeping became more complex. Regulations on types of annuities, for example, that seminaries can seek from donors has pressed some seminaries to add attorneys to their development offices. Regulations pertaining to scholarships for minority students, handicapped persons, international students, student loans, and scholarship aid in general have added even more layers to the administrative task of seminary staffs.

It should be underscored that while ecclesiastical pressures frequently joined those of civil authority in pushing for greater accessibility and affirmative action, faculties and administrations of theological schools tend to be uncommonly sensitive about these ethical issues. They do not want the government to have to tell them how to be just and fair; they want to be models for both the civil and ecclesial authorities. They push themselves on these issues even when not regulated by law.

We have noted that regulatory agencies related to the denominations, the academy, and the government had a serious impact upon the administration of theological education. This led to a mushrooming of both purposes and staff. Suddenly, presidents of seminaries not only had to use the corporate model to organize and run their institutions, but also had to practice entrepreneurship in seeking to survive. The office was not what it once was.

Robert Wister's history of the developments among Roman Catholics since 1965 reflects in many ways similar patterns.[22]   After experiencing a surge of students and a rapidly growing church following World War II, the number of persons offering themselves for priesthood began to drastically decline in 1965. Many schools had to close. Orders of nuns and lay brothers who once assisted with the chores of the school are gone. Faculty members are no longer exclusively priests working for meager salaries; they are lay persons with families; they belong to the same guilds as do other professors; they must be paid comparable wages. The number of priests qualified to teach in seminaries is declining and some who are qualified prefer to teach in departments of religion in universities, and thus are unavailable for appointment to theological schools. In addition, the search for faculty in Roman Catholic seminaries has become further complex as some schools try to find qualified women and minorities.

The rector no longer can simply depend on the bishop to find students and money. He must travel, visiting "sending bishops" to assure them that the school he represents does a good job of preparing persons for the priesthood. He must also find funds, especially in light of the fact that most Roman Catholic schools have little or no endowment. Added duties such as overseeing the development and business offices, which must meet the same auditing requirements as all other schools, require the rector to turn over to others the spiritual formation of students. This has become an area of specialization. The rector also has had to find a person to serve as academic dean, since he can no longer devote the hours needed to that task. Field education has flourished in these seminaries for the first time, calling for supervision. During the 1960s Roman Catholic schools also began to seek accreditation through the ATS, thus adding to their administrative work. In sum, the addition of professional staff, the financial situation, and the need for students have shifted the position of rector to one of supervision, administration, and fund raising. This is not to suggest the rector is no longer responsible for the overall health and well-being of the institution, but illustrates how the job has altered over the years due to changes in the church and in the world.

> The administration of theologates has changed, in most cases, from a simple system, in which a rector was responsible for virtually all aspects of the school to a more complex and expanded administrative structure involving many more individuals...During the process of change in administrative structures, the role of rector/president has seen the most extensive redefinition. It has evolved from a largely internal and comprehensive role to one in which internal responsibilities have been delegated to others and the rector/president himself has assumed more external responsibilities.[23]

In many Roman Catholic schools, the CEO now is called the rector/president or the president/rector.

Many Roman Catholic institutions have moved into lay education, special programs in spirituality or liturgy, and other such means of both serving the church and finding revenue.[24] Some of the smaller institutions also have banded together to form a "union" to conserve resources. In these unions, several schools work together to maintain a library and to share faculty and classroom space, though most continue to offer their own degrees and are responsible for the spiritual formation of their students. The head of these unions is generally called *president*. Since the conclusion of Vatican Council II in 1965, Roman Catholic schools have developed tremendously creative approaches in preparing persons for ministry, have endured considerable retrenchment and declines in students, and have engendered new possibilities for sharing ministry with professional laity. And as Katarina Schuth notes

> The "market," or "consumer," mentality is a strong driving force in determining the missions of theologates; to ensure enrollment, schools must try to provide programs that are responsive to the needs and goals of the bishops and religious superiors who support them, not always the same programs that faculty and administration believe are the best preparation for ministry.[25]

The changes in the life of denominations, the Roman Catholic Church, and the world have pressed seminaries to become entrepreneurs, to find new ways of generating both students and funds. The president has become the manager of this enterprising though small corporation.

As a consequence of these changes, presidents of every type of theological school tend to be more involved in organizing their institutions, managing larger staffs than in earlier times, specializing in fund raising, and seeking to maintain relationships with the cadre of persons needed to sustain the institution.

CONCLUSION

Even this brief summary of changes that have taken place in the presidency should make the reader conscious of how theological education, like human life, has grown more complex and more highly organized over the years. Simply being part of a community and dealing with its building codes, flow of traffic, historical preservation societies, sanitation laws, rent control, workers' compensation laws, and all the rest make operating a seminary very different from what it was when Andover opened its doors in 1808.

Early presidents spent their time teaching, moderating faculty meetings, sharing occasionally with trustees, and seeing that necessary details for maintaining common life were carried out. The job was academic and pastoral in nature.

From the late 1800s to the early 1900s, when churches and universities were moving toward corporate models of organization, seminaries were just beginning to consider the position of president. When presidents were appointed they had only small "mom and pop" shops to manage. Some of these "one-man rule" presidents did much to strengthen their institutions, despite the distasteful side effects. Many were distinguished churchmen who held responsible positions in their traditions and went on to be elected to higher church offices, such as bishop. They are best described as powerful, active churchleaders.

After 1945, both Protestant and Catholic schools grew with great rapidity, as did the churches. As life became more complex, the corporate model gradually became more appropriate. But the late 1960s and early 1970s brought many changes in the life of the church. The need for clergy declined for a season; enrollments fell off; and denominational bureaucracies were no longer providing many services formerly offered to churches. Presidents had to become more entrepreneurial in their approach to finding students and markets for graduates, in creating new programs to attract other types of students, and in using extension schools to take the seminary to people who could not come to the home location. This market-driven orientation has raised afresh the question of the basic purpose of theological institutions. Likewise, the press of so many diverse types of duties raises the question of the identity of the president.

NOTES

[1] Erskine Clarke uses these categories of interaction in *Leadership: The Study of the Seminary Presidency in Protestant Theological Seminaries*, vol. xxxii, Supplement II, 1995, of *Theological Education* (Association of Theological Schools: Pittsburgh, PA, 1995), 1. In a similar vein, Robert Wister and Joseph White have written about the development of the office of rector or rector-president in the Roman Catholic tradition, *Leadership: The Study of the Seminary Presidency in Catholic Theological Seminaries*, vol. xxxii, Supplement I, 1995, of *Theological Education* (Association of Theological Schools: Pittsburgh, PA, 1995). Earlier studies of the histories of theological schools that are also helpful include Glen Miller's *Piety and Intellect* (Atlanta: Scholars Press, 1990) and James W. Fraser, *Schooling the Preachers: The Development of Protestant Theological Education in the United States 1740-1875* (Lanham: University Press of America, 1988).

[2] Miller argues this case persuasively in Chapter 4 of *Piety and Intellect*, 67ff.

[3] Joseph M. White, op. cit., 5.

[4] T. Hartley Hall, IV, "The Lower Gifts", 4. A paper presented by President Hall at the opening convocation of Union Theological Seminary in Virginia, September 9, 1987.

[5] Robert Wister, op. cit., 58-60.

[6] The McLean article was discovered in the archives of Pacific School of Religion. It was bound with other printed addresses by Dr. McLean. This quotation is found on page 20.

[7] McLean, op. cit., 11.

[8] Laurence Veysey,*The Emergence of the American University*. (Chicago: The University of Chicago Press, 1965). "The term `administration,' as it came into use, referred to the president, deans, business staff, and often to a number of senior professors who regularly supported the president's wishes. More than this, however, `administration' connoted a certain state of mind; it meant those people in the university who characteristically thought in terms of institutional management or of organizational planning. Thus although American colleges had had presidents ever since the seventeenth century, administration represented a genuinely new force after the Civil War." 305.

[9] Wister, op. cit., 59.

[10] Robert Kelly. *Theological Education in America*.(New York: George H. Doran Co. 1924), 41. Italics mine.

[11] William Rainey Harper,"Shall the Theological Curriculum Be Modified, and How?" *The American Journal of Theology*, vol. III, no. 1, Jan. 1899, 45-66.

[12] William Adams Brown, Mark A. Mays, et al. *The Education of American Ministers*. 4 volumes.(New York: Institute of Social and Religious Research, 1934.)

[13] Kelsey puts these studies into the context of the current debate concerning the theological curriculum in *To Understand God Truly*, 93.

[14] H. Richard Niebuhr, Daniel Day Williams and James M. Gustafson. *The Advancement of Theological Education: The Summary Report of a Mid-Century Study*. (New York: Harper and Brothers, 1957), 45-7.

[15] Wister, op. cit., 51-63.

[16] I am drawing heavily in this section from Craig Dykstra and James Hudnut-Beumler, "The National Organizational Structures of Protestant Denominations: An Invitation to a Conversation." *The Organizational Revolution: Presbyterians and American Denominationalism*, edited by Milton J. Coalter, John M. Mulder, Louis B. Weeks. Louisville: Westminster/John Knox Press, 1992, 307-331. See especially 318ff.

[17] Dykstra and Hudnut-Beumler, op. cit., 319.

[18] Robert Wuthnow. *The Restructuring of American Religion* (Princeton: Princeton University Press, 1988).

[19] Dykstra and Hudnut-Beumler, op. cit., 321.

[20] Robert Wuthnow. op.cit.

[21] David H. Kelsey, *Between Athens and Berlin*,(Grand Rapids: Eerdmans, 1993), 84-86.

[22] Wister, op. cit.

[23] Katarina Schuth, *Reason for the Hope: The Future of Roman Catholic Theologates* (Wilmington: Michael Glazier, Inc., 1989), 83.

[24] George Schner, S. J., offers an interesting discussion of the emergence of laity as professional church workers in such fields as Christian education, sacred music, counseling. This has raised afresh the question of educating these people along with persons who are preparing for priesthood or of developing separate institutions and curricula. *Education for Ministry: Reform and Renewal in Theological Education*.(Kansas City: Sheed and Ward, 1993.)

[25] Katarina Schuth, op. cit., 46-47.

3

WHAT DO PRESIDENTS DO?

We have glimpsed something of the historical changes in the office of president of theological schools, and turn now to a description of what presidents in the current scene actually do with their time and energy. This will be a composite description of activities, as the uniqueness of each institution, its president, and its setting will refine what is sketched here with a very broad brush. We may refer to it as a job description, but in reality presidents feel they are involved in an unrelenting flow of events that no description could ever fully capture. The constant pressure of demands never ceases to surprise new presidents and confound even seasoned veterans.

Historically, it appears a president's job is shaped by interaction of the internal demands of the school and the external pressures from ecclesiastical and academic groups, governmental bodies, and local communities. The functions vary as the organizational models shift, as denominational structures are altered, as state and federal governmental bodies issue new regulations. Like most institutions in a society, theological schools reflect their context. The host culture provides models for the institution's organization and influences its modus vivendi. Denominational organizations or structures, which are themselves shaped in part by the culture in which they exist, are part of the sociocultural setting of theological schools and contribute to the shaping of these institutions. This is not to suggest that seminaries are simply at the mercy of social pressures. On the contrary, their own ethos, needs, purposes, and key individuals interact with the cultural setting. It is just this interplay that gives shape to the office of the president, as well as many other aspects of a school's life.

Clearly, over the years shifting organizational models and the complexity of society have meant the *adding* of duties which the CEO is expected to fulfill or have carried out by someone on his staff. To state the case simplistically, the job has slowly evolved from that of teacher/educator who helped manage family duties, to distinguished church executive who ran one of the tradition's prized educational institutions, to entrepreneur who struggles with diverse elements inside the schoolhouse and seeks support outside of it. At present, most people, including many presidents, think presidents are involved in almost every conceivable activity except education.[1]

Several things might be said about the numerous demands placed on the president. First is the incessant flow of demands that overpower newcomers to the office. Even though some of these persons occupied high pressure positions previously, most agree that they did not experience such heavy demands. Second, new presidents feel they are totally reactive; they are simply responding to requests, schedules, and regulations of others. They sense that they have totally lost control of their time. And finally, the buzzing chaos created by these constant pressures and deadlines makes it difficult to envision what one is about, to grasp the nature or identity of one's own work. I hope the categorization of activities listed in this chapter and in other places in the book, as well as the conceptualization of the office offered in the following chapter, will help with these problems.

My intent at this point is to list rather briefly some of the many duties in which most presidents engage, though no apportionment of time is suggested. Some of the duties will bear a few lines of explanation while others will be simply mentioned and elaborated upon at some later point in the book. The purpose is to familiarize the reader with how the evolution we observed in the last chapter has altered the nature of the president's work. In addition, I am deliberately leaving out certain duties because I wish to discuss them in greater detail in the following chapter. The present list is sufficient to indicate the accumulation of activities thrust upon the office in our time.

PRESIDENTIAL ACTIVITIES

The following discussion focuses on activities in which most presidents engage and also includes terms and phrases that describe *how* presidents do these things. As we move into this discussion, Clark Kerr's observation is helpful:

These multiple-constituency leaders are politicians who also administer, administrators who also preach, preachers who also must balance accounts, accountants of finance who must simultaneously balance the books of personal relations, human affairs accountants who must survive today tomorrow, planners of the future whose own careers have an uncertain future. They are the glue that holds their communities together, the grease that reduces friction among the moving parts, and the steering mechanism that guides any forward motion.[2]

1. Administrator. There is a mountain of literature dealing with administration, or management, or leadership, or some combination of these terms. I wish to use the term in this context to point to the task of the legal responsibility entrusted to the president to supervise the conduct of the life of an institution. Let us assume administration is the oversight of the entire operation, a component of the governance of the school. A part of administration is *management*. By this term I refer to attention to the routine functions that must be performed in any organization. Management is ordinarily thought of as following policies in an orderly fashion so everyone in the organization can "count on things" to operate as expected and needed. While the president should take part in formulating the administrative policies used by managers, no chief executive officer can manage every aspect of the seminary. That person is, however, responsible for seeing that every part of the institution is managed and managed well. The president is the "chief manager."

An administrator is also an *organizer*. Every institution has to have some form of organization. It may be hierarchical; it may be collegial or based on consensus making, but an institution has to have a structure. The various pieces must fit together and responsibilities distributed. Facets of the institution's life are divided up in such fashion that those responsible can relate to one another when needed and yet clearly have their own areas of accountability. How an institution is organized depends on many factors: the ethos of the school, the personality of the president, the legal charter or bylaws, the style of the denomination which owns the school, the requirements of the university of which it is a part, the nature of the academic programs. The person primarily responsible for organizing an academic institution is the president. The CEO may do this single-handedly, with colleagues, or according to ecclesial tradition or university patterns, but the president is the one who sees that it is done.

The president as administrator is also the *integrator* who must see that all of the pieces fit together and that the institution has integrity. The chief administrator must also be a *planner*. It is possible to have an enormously complicated planning process, or one can have a simple, oft revised plan for the future. Planners do not claim to know the future, but to project what they believe will happen and what will have to be done if the institution is to accomplish the goals it has set for itself.

To accomplish these various duties, a president must enlist the cooperation, ideas, and energies of trustees, faculty, staff, and students. To make all of these things happen requires that many people invest themselves in the work of the school. To accomplish this is the exercise of *leadership*. Enabling the entire community to move toward agreed upon goals or vision is the work of the leader/president.

2. Pastor. It is surprising how many presidents of theological schools think of themselves as pastors. This distinguishes them from their colleagues in colleges and universities. Just as a pastor of a church administers an institution, so a president is pastor/administrator and is frequently seen as the key *leader of worship,* especially in certain traditions. A president often stands for or represents the ecclesiastical tradition of the school. As a primary link with the church structure, the president serves as an *interpreter of the denomination,* communicating to individuals and the community what this or that action by the governing body means or offering advice on whether a given person will be able to be ordained by the particular tradition. The president becomes the *personal pastor* to individual students, faculty, staff, trustees, and supporters. Because of the numerous relationships which they enjoy, presidents often share in weddings, funerals, baptisms, ordinations, and other pastoral functions.

Some presidents indicate that, as pastors, they must serve as *disciplinarian.* The president is often the one delegated to tell a person: this kind of moral behavior is inappropriate in our community. She must share with a staff member the negative performance evaluations of others. She may have to ask someone to leave, whether student, staff, or faculty. Most of this in done in a pastoral fashion, though the ever-growing tendency for lawsuits is changing the tenor of these relationships. Presidents do not talk or write much about this dimension of their role, but it is part of the larger picture. That seminary presidents think of this duty as pastoral rather than administrative may also be unusual.

A president is a pastor who is a confidant, a friend, a counselor, a liturgist, a churchperson, and a disciplinarian.

3. Leader. This aspect will occupy considerable time and space in our exposition of the presidency. For now, let us agree that *leadership is a*

relationship. One leads when one persuades others to agree with a direction or position; one leads as one helps a group focus on its goals and expand them. Implied in what has been said is the role of the president as the *articulator of the goals*, the one who leads the educational community in defining its goals and then in stating these for all constituencies—both internal and external—to hear and understand. Some go further and think of themselves as the one who must *set the tone*, create the texture of the environment through style and manner. The president symbolizes the mode of life and work of the school.

While it may be true the president alone should not determine the goals of the institution, the president is the person who sees the entire institution in its context more clearly than anyone else, since the president is the only one who works with all of the constituencies. Therefore we should expect the president to be a *dreamer of dreams*, a person of vision and hope. Here one must be careful; dreams that are far removed from the realities of the institution can only cause frustration and confusion. Dreams that are rooted in the concrete historical situation have the possibility of flowering. To be able to distinguish between these types of dreams is part of leadership.

The leader is the *visible one*, the one who is watched by both insiders and outsiders. What does this school stand for? What kind of integrity is represented here? Where is the place going? While no president can decide all of these things alone, the president is the embodiment of the institution and its purposes. The word *embodiment* is used advisedly; it can be taken to mean that the president must be a productive scholar, a splendid administrator, an outstanding fund raiser. This unwarranted expectation produces frustration for the person in the office as well as for other sectors of the community. But if embodiment means the CEO reflects the basic commitments and values of the institution, then it makes sense, for the president is the symbol of the school.

4. Financier. Whether dean, rector, or principal, the chief executive officer of an institution must deal with money. In most cases this person is a *fund raiser*, a person who talks with others, whether individuals or foundations, about funding a specific aspect of the school's work. The presence or lack of professional development staff makes a significant difference in the time and style of this particular work. But there is no question the president is the chief fund raiser.

Just as important, however, is the *management of funds* that have already been given to the institution. The president ordinarily does not deal directly with investing funds, though in situations where the endowment is small, this responsibility is occasionally added. Trustee groups or professional investment services generally handle details of investing, but the president is usually present at meetings, consulted on the ethics of investment policies, and must be sensitive to the fluctuation of the endowment since its income will affect the next year's budget. Essential to management of funds is being sure that the auditors (and/or the government) will find the books in order. Donors expect that their funds are being used for the purpose for which they were given. Trustees want to make sure there will be no embezzlement of funds. As in the case of the development work, having a professional staff in the business office helps, but the chief executive officer of a small institution still has close contact with the monies. One research study suggests that presidents of small schools usually are expected to have more financial knowledge than their counterparts in larger institutions.[3]

Finally, the president is caught between those with the urge to spend now and those who want to preserve capital for the future. It is not uncommon to have pressure from trustees to reduce spending for the sake of the future while faculty, staff, and students want to enlarge the budget to meet pressing demands of the day. The president, supported by the board, one hopes, must "give voice to the most voiceless: the next generation," as one president notes. Both groups are fulfilling their responsibilities; one is seeking to make things better now and the other is concerned with the viability of the institution for future generations. The president is in the middle actually developing a *budget*. One does not ordinarily develop a budget in isolation from the cost centers or the heads of various areas of the school's life—such as academic, building and grounds, personnel. Though teamwork may be involved in budget building, it is the president who is accountable for final decisions about what will be funded and what will not. After this, comes monitoring, to ensure the budget is not exceeded. Keeping abreast of the multifaceted financial situation is a constant.

5. Connector. A president who recently retired writes:

> Although I found being the president of a seminary a lonely job, it was a job that depended on connections with others. The ability to build these connections is at the heart of what the job is about.

One could use the expression *boundary person* to describe the role of connector more accurately, for the president is always on the boundary between the school and the rest of the world as well as between groups within the institution. As we have seen, the CEO interacts with financial investors, persons in the local business community, with churches, the university, alumni/ae, donors, accrediting associations, the local city council, special interest groups, and many more. All of these groups are connected with the school for different reasons. The president is also the link between students and trustees, staff and trustees, faculty and staff.

In this role the president is an *interpreter* of the school to the many constituencies and also the one who seeks to interpret other groups to the faculty, staff, and students. The president is not the only one doing this, but the role demands that the CEO be the key spokesperson. Getting around to visiting with these groups means the president is a *traveler*, one who has to attend the meetings of ecclesiastical bodies and accrediting commissions and visit with donors or potential givers who may live many miles away. The number of meetings at which the president is expected to be present is amazing. But many times these groups or their representatives come to the campus and must be entertained. So presidents, and in many cases their spouses, are *entertainers;* their homes are frequently opened to alumni/ae groups, donors, trustees, and other friends of the institution. They in turn are entertained in other people's homes and clubs; this is seen as part of the work of a president. It is nurturing the institution's family. It is not merely a matter of raising funds, it is building support for the institution; it is fostering friends who help the school in so many ways; it is repaying persons who have been gracious toward this particular community of faith.

6. An Ecumenical Person. Because of their office, presidents associate with persons from other traditions. But there is some evidence that people selected to occupy the office have a natural openness to others, or, are ecumenical "by nature." It is interesting to note how many current and former presidents state that one of their goals was to help their institution live more fully in the life of the larger church, to be less provincial, more open to God's work among other traditions. Others said sharing in the work of the ATS enabled them to develop deep friendships with persons from other traditions; they learned from one another. A person who shared in this study, but had not known seminary presidents previously, observed that all of the ones she dealt with were committed to working *ecumenically* wherever possible. In some cases, this has meant getting charter changes to allow faculty members to come from outside the denomination that owned the institution; in other situations, it involved exchange programs, visiting faculty or lecturers. In still other cases, cooperative unions or programs

were developed with other schools. Presidents as a group appear to be persons who are aware of God's larger flock.

It was a group of presidents, concerned about the provincial nature of churches and seminaries, that undertook to make their ATS colleagues more sensitive to our global village and its impact on theological education in North America. Accreditation requirements now mandate that each institution be engaged in *globalization*. These presidents were ecumenists, for they encouraged those involved in theological education to reflect on what the peoples of Africa and Asia, for example, have to tell us about ministry.

As the preceding illustration makes clear, presidents must assume responsibility for the advancement of the enterprise of theological education. The ATS is composed of presidents and deans who work together to assure that appropriate standards are in place for evaluating seminaries, for stimulating new educational programs or degrees, for finding support for faculty sabbatics, and putting in place research projects—all for the sake of *advancing the profession*. Presidents, by virtue of their office, are the persons strategically located to nurture the health and well-being of the enterprise.

7. Combatant. Reading any one of the histories of theological education reminds us that controversies have always been part of the seminary scene. The first seminary, Andover, experienced such a serious dispute among the faculty that trustees had to request the president to bring peace. Students turned on presidents and all but destroyed institutions over the slavery issue. In the early part of this century Princeton Seminary experienced a major controversy which led to the founding of another school. The Lutherans had a serious fight over doctrine which led to splitting their seminary in St. Louis. More recently, the Southern Baptists have fired several presidents and a number of faculty over doctrinal matters.

Disagreements can be fearsome when opposing parties claim God's blessing. Leaders in the Roman Catholic Church differed as to what it meant to follow the guidance of Vatican II; faculties were split and many took great exception to the views of some rectors, to say nothing of bishops. There are controversies among faculty within an institution, between the school and the denomination, between factions within the denomination, any of which may be represented in the school. Students were actively involved in trying to get institutions to change during the 1960s, but theological students had been doing this for a century. The basis for the disagreements may be theological or social, but the consequences can be deleterious for a school. In more recent times seminaries have experienced sharp attacks from numerous caucuses, each representing a different position and making demands.

Presidents are *persons of controversy*. They know about contention firsthand. They are frequently the ones who are targeted and removed from office. Or, perhaps worse, they have to live with the controversy week after week. This reality adds stress and distress to the job. Fortunately, not all presidents are in the eye of these storms.

8. Person of Faith. This category refers to activities that most presidents engage in due in part to the nature of the office. Presidents are driven to the roots of their own faith and calling. They sense the spiritual nature of their task both in its problems and possibilities. Many report they have become engaged in *spiritual disciplines* more seriously than before. They read their Bibles, attend worship, pray, and participate in social action to keep their own commitments lively. The pressures of the job cause them to think about and then rethink their own *sense of calling*. What has God called me to do? Why am I in this place at this time? How is my ministry being expressed in this position? What is it that I can do from my position that no one else in the institution can do? To find time for such disciplined worship and devotion is difficult, but presidents tell us it is a part of their lives.

9. This last category is intended to add a few additional terms that persons familiar with the office find descriptive. For instance, *loner*, which may have negative connotations for some, is a term frequently used to describe the weight of final decisions resting on this person's shoulders, regardless of how many others share in the decision-making process. Or, it can refer to the isolation one experiences after making an unpopular decision. As one president wrote:

> Maybe the greatest gift the Seminary gave me was the capacity to stand alone when I needed to stand alone. It was here that I began to experience in a way I had never known before the difference between loneliness and solitude. As Paul Tillich once wrote,"loneliness is the pain of being alone; solitude is the joy of being alone;" it is in solitude that we are led to the deep wells of our faith. Conflict and isolation are part and parcel of the life of a seminary president ... Learning to make this work for you is the key not only to effectiveness, but to longevity in the job.

In our litigious society, a CEO sometimes feels like an *attorney* because of the laws and lawsuits that are part of the work. One also becomes a *seismologist*, in that the shifts in the environment shake an entire institution;

presidents have to interpret and deal with these events. At the close of Vatican II, reality shifted for any number of rectors; when the Lutheran denominations merged some years ago, the playing field was suddenly realigned. Congressional changes in the tax laws can create havoc with development efforts. Sensing changes and their meanings for educational institutions is all part of the job.

CONCLUSION

I have not offered a job description of a president so much as provided categories which enable the reader to have a composite picture of activities and terms that characterize what occupies the time and minds of persons in this office. What is missing, of course, is the detail: the nitty-gritty of dealing with a housing policy so that all are treated equally, the greeting of visiting Christians from China, the pain of visiting the hospital to see a student with AIDS, the trauma of learning that one of the school's major investments has crashed, the disappointment when a faculty member's contract cannot be renewed. But I hope we have prepared the way for an interpretation of these practices as crucial to the educational venture.

Classifying the activities and having a clear picture of the task does not necessarily help a president manage the constant flow of events. One thing that every president has to learn, however, is how to protect oneself, how to gain some control over one's time, and how to find space for reading, reflecting, and relaxing. There are certain events that must be attended and deadlines that absolutely must be met. But in between, there is discretionary time. There is no secret approach or method for taking control of one's schedule, so far as I know. Each person must consciously work at organizing things that must be done for the sake of the institution, eliminating other activities that are not so essential, and carving out time for self and family. It can be done!

As we move through the discussion, some of the roles discussed here will be explicated with greater care; others will be added to the list. But for the time being, these features give a sense of the nature of the job as one that never ends. Many presidents say they have had to come to terms with the feeling that one is never "off duty." The roles of the president penetrate into every cranny of a person's life. Yet presidents tell of their joy of sharing in the shaping of an institution's history, of their satisfaction in enriching ministry, of the deep personal friendships that have been theirs over the years, of the challenges that keep them young, and of the inveterate optimism that sustains them. Presidents tend to be people of hope; they expect to share in the dawning of grace.

NOTES

[1] "Books written during the past twenty years underscore a continuing trend: the office of president is seen as declining in educational significance while becoming more and more managerial...The question keeps recurring: Can the president lead as an educator, or is he or she merely an executive director managing one of many complex social organizations?" Louis T. Benezet, Joseph Katz, Frances W. Magnusson, *Style and Substance: Leadership and the College Presidency* (Washington,D. C.: American Council on Education, 1981), 2. It is also true that the influential writings of Clark Kerr do not use educational terms in describing the work of the president. See *Presidents Make a Difference: Strengthening Leadership in Colleges and Universities* (Washington,D. C.: The Association of Governing Boards, 1984); *The Uses of the University,* Third edition with a new preface and postscript (Cambridge, Mass: Harvard University Press, 1982). Kerr and Marian L. Gade, *The Many Lives of Academic Presidents: Time, Place, and Character* (Washington,D.C.: Association of Governing Boards, 1986). One must also note that seminaries are not large universities or colleges, which the foregoing studies focus upon. It is true, however, that even the presidents of small institutions have similar expectations placed upon them.

[2] Clark Kerr and Marion Gade, *The Many Lives of Presidents* (Washington, D. C.: Association of Governing Boards of Universities and Colleges, 1986), xiv.

[3] These and other suggestions are found in Howard Tuckman and Pat Arcady,"Myths about Size and Performance: Managing the Small College," *Educational Record*, vol.66, no. 3, (Summer, 1985), 16-30.

4

THE PRESIDENT AS EDUCATOR

In the first chapter of this study we noted Leon Pacala's warning that the presidency of theological institutions lacks any clear conceptualization. Next we observed that—throughout the history of the presidency—society, church, and the academy have shaped the office and placed numerous duties upon the occupant. Having listed a few of these many demands, it is easy to understand how occupants of the office and their constituencies envision presidents as harried administrators or as tired fund raisers. There is no conceptualization of the office that enables people to hold together these diverse activities. In general people do not visualize presidential activities as educational.

I wish to propose such a way of viewing the president; I believe it is helpful for all concerned to understand the president as an educator. This person is, after all, president of an *educational* institution, a *school*. In setting forth this view, it is necessary to define certain terms, specifically the words *education, practice,* and *teaching.* I shall not argue for the correctness of my definitions, though I believe this can be done; in each case I shall refer to others who have done so. My intent is to use existing definitions to offer an understanding of the presidency.

EDUCATION

The definition of education I will use is: *Education is the process designed by persons, accomplished through an institution, to enable students to think, know, feel, and choose.*[1] This definition states that education is an *intentional* activity done by persons with some goal in mind. Learning can take place by plan or by accident, but education is learning by design. One can learn something about uneven stairs by tripping and falling, but to refer to this behavior as an education is inappropriate. If every experience or bit of behavior is education, then education is simply experience. Our definition of the word suggests education is a deliberate activity, designed by a person or persons with some end in mind. It is a *process*, which means it consists of steps, units, stages, structures, and activities within those structures. A faculty member designs a course of study; the faculty as a whole designs a curriculum. Both are structured processes. Each involves several types of learning experiences, such as discussion, question and answer, reading and reflection. Education is *designed* by a person or persons; it is not accidental.

Education is *accomplished through an institution*. It may be a very simple institution—a tutor on one end of a log; or a highly complex one—the modern university. We commonly refer to such institutions as *schools* though they are not limited to such. The educational structures and processes have an *end* in mind; that is, students will be enabled to think, know, feel, and choose.

Using our definition, one can understand the theological school as an institution where we ordinarily assume the faculty is primarily responsible for designing the educational process for students who enroll in the institution. Even though persons like deans of students, trustees, church leaders, and graduates might contribute or share in some way, we still think of the faculty as the primary designers of the educational process. The president as a member of the faculty ordinarily shares in the designing. But I would suggest in addition that the actions of the board in establishing the stated purpose, the priorities of the budget set by the board and administration, the availability of space, and library and media resources are *essential ingredients of the educational design*; they contribute to the shape and substance of the educational process. And many of these latter items are more the prerogative of the president than the faculty. In other words, the president shares in designing the educational experience as a member of the faculty *and* as a trustee and administrator.

The faculty, with the president, designs learning experiences for the students. The president's role in these designs may involve participation in discussions about the curriculum as well as the financial and policy-making aspects of the design mentioned in the preceding paragraph. The president's work is not adjunctive to that of the faculty, nor is it simply that of enabling faculty to do educational work. His or her activities or "practices" are as endemic to the educational process as the activities of any other faculty member.

The *purpose* of the educational process designed for theological students has been the source of considerable debate in recent years. Though persons differ as to their version and vision of the purpose of theological education, one common understanding is that students should learn to think, know, feel, and choose with reference to the Christian faith. David Kelsey articulates this purpose or goal as "understanding God truly." To understand God truly involves thinking, knowing, feeling, and choosing. Readers may want to substitute their own version of the purpose.[2] I am using this particular one because it serves well to illustrate my argument. In saying this, I do not mean to suggest that just any goal will do. Kelsey deals with many inadequate goals and shows why they are so. It is not my purpose here, however, to engage in that discussion.

In addition to his or her role in the educational process for students, the president also designs other learning experiences for such groups as trustees, staff, faculty, and other constituencies. Obviously, the president does not act alone in these designs, but is the primary strategist even as the faculty is primary in designing educational processes for students. Both faculty and president are functioning as educators in the same institution. They are engaged in similar processes, as we shall see shortly.

Kelsey's work deals with the purpose of education designed for students. I would suggest that the institution's purpose, however one states it, becomes a part of the content of the education a president designs for the institution's constituencies. The educational processes designed by the president for the institution's various constituencies have as their purpose creating and nurturing the understanding of the seminary's vocation— epitomized in its statement of purpose—so that trustees, church and civic leaders, donors, and prospective students can think, know, feel, and choose in terms of theological education.

Thus the president collaborates with the faculty in designing education for seminary students, but is also engaged in designing educational experiences for the school's other constituencies as well. The degree to which a president's activities (sometimes viewed as buzzing chaos) are educational will become clearer as we discuss these activities or practices.

PRACTICES

When thinking of education in terms of institutions, the *concreteness* of the process seems self-evident: lectures, textbooks, classroom space, curricular designs, graduation requirements. These all are aspects of the historical reality that makes a school what it is today. They obviously are concrete components of the educational process. But when we think of the education of *a person*, there is a tendency to imagine the educational process as a phenomenon which happens mysteriously in the student's subjective experience as a professor lectures or engages the student in Socratic dialogue. Certainly, lectures and dialogue may generate thinking, knowing, feeling, or choosing. But we must not forget collateral reading, research papers, and evaluation of those papers by faculty; these concrete activities are also part of education. In addition, field education faculty remind us that sharing leadership in parish life and reflecting on it is a valid part of the learning experience.[3] A similar kind of structured learning is found in the clinical pastoral education designed for hospitals or other institutional settings. The point here is simply to underscore that the education of theological students and the education of the seminary constituencies clearly involve a diverse number of material objects, concrete settings, and a variety of resources, as well as subject matters. The educational process, whether for students or other constituencies, is thus both concrete and material.[4]

David Kelsey states the case well when he writes that

> the search for true understanding of God (the educational purpose of the school) is not a free-floating "educational process" that is relatively independent of a material base and independent of arrangements of social, economic, and political power... It (theological education) is not merely "contained" or "embodied" in institutions, a ghost in administrative machinery. "Theological education" is an aspect of a theological school, abstracted from the school's concrete practices which are inherently materially based, institutionalized, and socially situated.[5]

His assertions about the concreteness of education apply to the designs for seminary students as well as the education of the institution's other constituencies.

Kelsey's observations about the concreteness of the educational process are dependent upon his use of the word *practice*. He obviously is using it in a particular way. He defines the word as

> any form of socially established cooperative human activity that is complex and internally coherent, is subject to standards of excellence that partly define it, and is done to some end but does not necessarily have a product.[6]

The author explains each aspect of this definition with carefully developed and persuasive arguments. For my purposes here, I intend to use Kelsey's conclusions, not repeat his arguments. I am using practices to refer to those patterns of activities we refer to as teaching, or fund raising, or worship, or administration. Such activities are described in the Old and New Testaments, meaning, these practices have histories. People have been doing them for centuries. There are other practices that are of more recent origin, but nevertheless have histories.

As we state the case in this fashion, it becomes clear that practices are activities people ordinarily do together. Teaching, fund raising, worshiping, or administering are things done in or by groups. Folk cooperate in doing these things and follow given procedures, or rule-like regularities, as Kelsey calls them. Even when a solitary teacher uses the Socratic method with a student, she is in the company of teachers who have taught in this fashion over the centuries. This observation calls attention to the different ways of teaching, raising money, worshiping, or administering; each distinguishable because it has its own patterns or rules. Free, informal worship is not like highly structured, formal worship; the administration of an authoritarian is not like that of a consensus builder, but both have patterns that are inherent in their particular approach.

But regardless of which pattern of worship is used, it has a purpose. One might say that the purpose of worship is adoring and praising God. The purpose of teaching is enabling students to assess the truth. Are the practices accomplishing their purpose? How does one know this? A practitioner must constantly lift the question, must engage in critical reflection while worshiping or teaching, or raising funds.

From the examples I have used, it should be evident that faculty members and presidents are involved in numerous practices as they carry out the work of theological schools. To quote Kelsey once again,

> a theological school [is] a complex set of interrelated practices...The set will include practices of teaching and learning, practices of research, practices of governance of the school's common life, practices of maintenance of the school's resources, practices in which persons are selected for the student body and for the faculty, and practices in which students move through and then are deemed to have completed a course of study.[7]

Clusters of these practices compose the work of the president, as we noted in the preceding chapter. But why is this concept of *practice* and the notion of a theological school as an interrelated, complex set of practices important for understanding the president as educator? Why am I making an issues of this? First, the term assists us in understanding the educational process in all of its concreteness: lectures, specific personnel regulations, quizzes, financial audits, term papers, fund-raising efforts, classroom assignments, schedules of classes for a specific semester. Our tendency is to imagine that the intellectual activities of the classroom or library are expressions of the educational process, while forgetting these other equally vital activities. Kelsey reminds us that education is not something that happens "out there someplace" or even "in here someplace." It is not floating around in an intellectual realm.[8] It is, rather, quite material and concrete whether aimed at students within the school or other constituencies of the institution. The activities which presidents engage in daily as the primary focus of their work are concrete, educational practices.

Second, the use of the term *practice* helps us realize that not only worship and teaching have histories, but so have the practices of administration and fund raising. They are all part of the "tradition." In these particular cases, they can be found throughout church history. These are not simply "evils" of our present age or the intrusion of secular activities into the theological arena. Such activities have a long and honorable history in the Christian tradition, though they can become deformed and twisted as can the practice of worship. Using the concept of practice reminds us that presidents are engaged in the activities which belong to the historic ministry of God's people.

Third, to understand these presidential activities as practices helps us appreciate that some of these more "material" matters are as "intellectual" and "spiritual" as are scholarly research and worship. They are not accomplished without intelligence and they are a form of spiritual service. Kelsey argues persuasively that the distinction between "physical" or "natural" or "material" practices, on the one hand, and "spiritual" or "intellectual" practices on the other hand is to be rejected.[9] To classify the president's work as "inferior" or "busy-work," as distinguished from intellectual activity, or "material" rather than "spiritual" will not do. Presidential practices are forms of spiritual service.

Finally, the term "practice" helps us perceive the need to be self-critical, to engage in reflective criticism of every system and about every policy. Practices become institutionalized to some degree; this is as true of forms of worship as of administration. Having become institutionalized they are open to the distortions, pressures, and self-interest of those engaged in them. The ways we teach as well as our management style need to be constantly evaluated in terms of intrinsic purposes and the goals of the institution. Such scrutiny of one's own activities and those of the institution are surely one of the president's major concerns and inherent in the practices themselves.

Understanding presidential activities as practices enables us to see the president's role (1) as a participation in the educational process which is both concrete and material,(2) as a form of ministry rooted in the history of the Christian tradition, (3) as an intelligent expression of one's spiritual service, and (4) as demanding the same reflective criticism that should be present in all of the practices that constitute theological education.

Viewing theological education as a network of practices enables one to understand the roles of the president in other than administrative or management categories. This is not to deny the presence and importance of administration and management. It is rather to perceive them as *educational activities*. These particular activities borrow insights from the disciplines of management, administration, or organizational development—just as the professor of theology borrows categories from philosophy, or the pastoral care professor borrows insights from the discipline of psychology. The questions to ask are: Do the borrowed categories shape and determine the discipline or the practice? Are the insights from this or that school of management determining or shaping the purpose of the institution and its administration? Or, is the theological purpose of the school shaping both the administration and the teaching?

The practices a seminary president engages in are practices in the service of the institution's purpose. As such, they are endemic to the education offered by a theological school.

TEACHING

While the practices of governance, maintaining the school's resources, administration, and fund raising, are all part of education, teaching-learning practices are primary. While all of the practices are legitimately seen as dimensions of the educational process, the practices of teaching-learning are crucial and essential to the designs that enable persons to think, know, feel, and choose. Teaching, in other words, is the distinctive, the quintessential activity of education. While other activities can be seen as endemic to education, teaching is that without which education cannot take place.

If you ask presidents whether they teach, the response generally is cast in terms of offering a class for students within the seminary curriculum. Some presidents are almost apologetic that they no longer find time to offer a class or even keep abreast of their field of specialization. Most seminary presidents have Ph.Ds but only a few manage to read widely in their field and teach a class annually. Is there a sense in which we can say that presidents *do* engage in this most important educational practice, that of teaching?

We shall use a definition of teaching offered by Thomas Green, a philosopher of education. In his book, *The Activities of Teaching*, Green begins by first examining what teachers do. Since teaching involves many different activities, he uses three headings of classification. There are *institutional* acts (sending booklists to the library, keeping records, attending faculty meetings); *strategic* acts (evaluating, planning, motivating); and *logical* acts (explaining, concluding, giving reasons, defining).[10] All of these are activities of teaching, though Green would argue that the logical acts are the most essential ones for the act of teaching; teaching cannot go on without these activities. To a certain extent, this is true of the strategic acts, but teaching can take place without those institutional acts, though *in fact* it ordinarily does not. Think of these categories of activities as three concentric circles: the innermost consists of the logical acts, the next circle represents the strategic acts, and the outer circle the institutional acts. All are part of teaching, though some are more crucial than others.

I do not wish to trace Green's entire argument, but to examine his definition of teaching which is: the process of dealing with subject matter in such a way as to enable students to assess the truth of the same in terms of their own frames of reference.[11] The teacher, through various methods (assigning reading, lecturing, discussing), enables students to deal with subject matter (the theology of Augustine, the emotions of grief, the Greek language, urban sociology) in terms of their own frames of references (in a language they understand, using words that make sense to them, relating the subject matter to "their" world) so they can assess its truth (learn appropriate criteria for the subject matter, look at alternatives, evaluate claims).

The point of this discussion is to emphasize that presidents do engage in the activities of teaching. Many presidential actions involve institutional acts, while others are strategic or logical actions. A quick recall of the various practices in which presidents engage makes this abundantly clear. Therefore, let us restate Green's definition of teaching in terms of presidents. Teacher/

presidents, through various methods (assigning reading to staff or trustees, lecturing trustees or church judicatories, discussing with administrative staff), enable students (trustees, staff, donors, church leaders) to deal with subject matter (faith and learning, the purpose of the seminary, the ethical implications of admission policies, the impact of governmental regulations on church bodies, the ethics of investing) in terms of their own frames of references (in a language they understand, using words that make sense to them, relating the subject matter to "their" world) so they can assess its truth (learn appropriate criteria for the subject, look at alternatives, evaluate claims).

Using this definition of teaching allows us to see that presidents who do not have a regular offering in the curriculum do nonetheless teach, though perhaps not in traditional settings. They teach in *unconventional classrooms*. They spend many hours with trustees, teaching them about the institution, peculiarities of theological education, issues before the churches, changes in our society, or the nature of shared governance in educational institutions. Presidents teach (as well as learn from) staff members and faculty. They gather resources for these sessions; they frequently use films and other educational supports. As they visit among the constituencies, presidents teach congregations and individuals about theological education and the place of learning in the life of the church and faith. They do this with great intentionality as part of their fund raising. People must come to appreciate what theological schools do or they will never support them; their thinking, knowing, feeling, and choosing theological schools as recipients of their gifts is dependent upon this educational process. Fund raising can be seen as primarily an educational activity.

It may be true that presidents do not spend an inordinate number of hours in the library reflecting on manuscripts, but they do reflect on the *institution as text* as well as read many different types of material. They ponder the meaning of events within the history and current life of an institution in an effort to divine the purpose and nature of the school. They read historical documents as well as current committee reports from trustees and faculty. A president who is reflective and intentional about these realities can make an ordinary committee meeting into a meaningful learning experience for all.

The president has a teaching role analogous to that of a faculty member. Both have subject matter, though it differs; and both deal with learners, though mostly different learners. But both are engaged in the activities of teaching; they participate in the ministry of teaching.

PRESIDENT AS ACADEMICIAN

It seems clear that presidents share in designing educational processes for students and other constituencies. Furthermore, presidents engage in the central activity of the educational process, that is teaching. Yet in our earlier listing of the duties of presidents, little mention was made of academic activities; the duties and expectations given were taken from reports of presidents. In fact, many presidents believe they do not contribute significantly to the educational programs of their own schools. Using our new insights, I want to discuss the academic role of the president and give examples of leadership in that area. Next, I will reclassify the practices of the president, using different terminology to locate those practices within the new conceptualization of the office.

In the earlier listing, activities dealing with academic leadership were omitted. This was done, as we have noted, because both the presidents writing for this project and presidents of institutions of higher education say they do not see themselves as having a great deal to do with the academic side of the institution. Yet presidents are involved in practices which constitute the educational experience offered to those within the institution as well as those outside of it. They share in committee work with the faculty, the academic vice president, the board, and the students in areas where key academic decisions are made. Presidents frequently are vocal participants in curricular discussions, when designs are being shaped that set learning experiences for students. With the governing board, they share in policy making that determines what is taught and how. They are usually key in the practice of calling new faculty. They share in developing an annual budget with staff members; in many ways, the budget shapes the educational process. More will be said about this concept of shared leadership since it is at the heart of educational institutions, but at this point I am emphasizing that the president is one of the educators who designs as well as one of the teachers who carries out the educational process of a theological school—keeping in mind that some of this education is aimed at students and some is designed for other constituencies. This, I believe, is a more adequate way of interpreting the educator/president's "academic leadership."

Robert Lynn is fond of using the phrase *intellectual leadership* in addition to academic leadership, or as a part of it. By this he means the president's intellectual task of reflecting on the institution in its wholeness and discerning matters about the school and the world that need to be brought into the conversation of the community. These are matters, he believes, which may not be attended to if the president does not focus on them. The president, by his very position, is pressed to think about the school in light of the state of the church; the place of religion in academic institutions in general; the place of scholarship in the theological institution; the sociocultural context including the economic, social, and political environment; and the immediate limitations of budget and personnel resources.

To be specific, because of practices presidents are engaged in daily, they have the opportunity to raise ethical questions about the adequacy of the school's programs for carrying out the institution's purpose, the ethics of investment policies and employment practices, justice for equal work done (Is the director of maintenance on a par with the chef and the director of continuing education?), admission practices, and a host of others. The ethics of higher education is frequently a neglected subject unless raised by the CEO. One president, serving on the executive committee of his regional accrediting agency, was instrumental in focusing the region's annual meeting on the ethics of higher education. The students on this occasion were presidents and deans of institutions of higher education in a major segment of the United States.

The president may be the one who raises the question of living out the institution's history in this particular time. Can or should the institution become something totally different? The historical dimensions of a school's life are crucially important if it is to retain its focus, or even refocus its efforts. In what unique ways can this particular institution serve the church and the world at this juncture of its life? What does it mean for the school that religious scholarship has shifted from the seminary to the university? The task of the president in assisting the community to reflect on its goals involves both history and the continuing struggle with the purpose of theological schools.

The president may raise the question of organization with staff members. Can the school's very style of organization make it a learning organization; that is, one in which all who work within the school are encouraged to continue to learn?[12] The style of organization can serve as a teacher to the community. The practices of administration and management are not unrelated to the role of teacher/educator.

These represent some of the intellectual challenges and educational opportunities facing presidents. This is not something added to a president's list of duties; it is a way of viewing the numerous tasks of the president and an approach to handling them.

Is such intellectual leadership taking place or is this merely a wish? A member of the Graduate Faculty of Business at Columbia University who has taught presidents of seminaries as well as CEOs from other not-for-profit institutions for a number of years, was asked if he could point to anything distinct about these presidents. He replied that as a group they were better read and more sensitive to social issues than were presidents from other not-for-profits. Part of the president's scholarship is to struggle with the *intellectual and social issues* of our time. What is individualism doing to the shape of faith in our society and especially to church members? Is Christianity able to contribute to one's identity in this day and time? What does it mean when denominations appear to be fading from the religious scene? Should ecclesiastical institutions be taxed? What does the emergence of the postmodern era mean for Christian faith and scholarship?

Such academic leadership is not limited to the institutions in which presidents work. They are teacher/educators to their larger communities. During the civil rights struggles of the 1960s, the dean along with colleagues of a university divinity school acted as a catalyst to educate the entire university and move it toward a more responsible stance. Another divinity school's dean and faculty played a major role in helping their university deal with the ethics of investing its endowment. Through their published works, they educated trustees and administrators throughout North America.

The same is true with respect to the denomination which governs the seminary. Out of concern for how the currents of our time have shaped and/or de-formed his denomination, one president was instrumental in inaugurating a major study of the denomination in an effort to help the church find its roots and identity in today's world.

Another illustration depicts how presidents work to change the enterprise of theological education. A group of presidents became concerned that more seminaries seemed to flounder because of poor administration than lack of funds. By working with a foundation, and later the ATS, they established an institute that operated for a number of years to educate CEOs into the mysteries of administration, planning, and finance.

The point of these stories is to underscore the fact that presidents are educators who seek to bring about change within the enterprise of theological education, the churches, and the world. Pressures of the office do not always leave adequate time for these activities, but various universities, ecumenical councils, denominations, and the ATS are not the same today because of the educational work of some presidents. These presidents not only "run" seminaries, they help create and reclaim institutions in our larger society. Being a president is more than simply managing one's own shop.

ACTIVITIES AS PRACTICES

Perhaps we are now in a position to cluster the plethora of activities which compose the daily round of presidents into groups of practices. By offering new groupings of these practices, we may more clearly see them as the practices of education and ministry. The suggested clustering which follows may help bring order to the chaos created by a multitude of activities. The reader may envision other ways of classifying them, or moving some from one category to another, but the point of the exercise will nonetheless be clear.

1. The teaching/learning practices. They are deliberately placed first in the list because of their importance. The educator/president's gathering of resources, teaching, and sharing in setting policies that shape the institution are of primary importance. The matter of setting policies should be underscored again, for whether it is board, faculty, or administrative policies, they are the "institutionalization" of values crucial to a community's teaching and learning. Policies reflect the governance of the institution. Just as significant will be the questions a president raises concerning the impact of modern technology on the educational process, or the educational validity of becoming an extension school, or a host of other such questions.

2. Deaconal practices. Like the institutional activities of teaching, there are a series of activities involved in maintaining the institution and providing services needed for the common life; they are part of the education that goes on in the seminary. This includes activities of the building and grounds committee which provides classroom space and faculty offices; the finance and investment committee that gathers resources and sees they are managed prudently; and the business office which oversees providing food, telephones, copy machines. These and many other activities of management and governance fall into the deaconal category.

But one must also include services rendered by the president in the community, such as serving on the United Fund Committee, or the regional accrediting agency; for here she is also teaching and engaging in education.

3. Pastoral practices. Presidents are pastors to individuals in and out of the school. As a pastor, the president must sometimes exercise discipline and deal with controversy, as do all educators. But for our discussion, we need to underscore the significance of personnel matters. Educational institutions are labor intensive; that is, most of what happens in these schools has to do with people. Whether it be staff or faculty, students or board members, personnel matters occupy a major place in the president's agenda. There are personnel policies and procedures which should be carried out with care, justice, and sensitivity. Most of the relationships with faculty belong here. The president should not be the personal counselor to faculty members, but rather attend to the processes of their calling, clarity of their duties, salaries, benefits, support system, and retirement arrangements.

4. Practice of witness. As we have seen, one of the president's duties is to articulate the vision which belongs to the community. As an educator, the president probably has more opportunity to do this than anyone else; by doing it well, the president can help unify the community, and assist it in clarifying its mission and rediscovering its purpose. The president witnesses to these matters to the school itself, but also to denominations, accrediting groups, and the local community of merchants and homeowners. Even in the planning process, the president is able to witness to the purpose for which the institution exists and thus assist in maintaining continuity with the past while moving into the future.

5. Practices of apologetics. This word is not used as much as it was in Christian conversation in earlier times. We do not ordinarily *defend* our doctrines or theological positions today, though some believe we should.[13] I am using the term here to suggest that much of the president's work as a "public relations" person is that of presenting to the general public, the denominations, or churches the case for the theological seminary. He is defending the institution; giving reasons why the school contributes to the health of the church; showing how theological education makes an impact on the general public through the graduates and the scholarly work of the faculty. But in a special way, the president is practicing apologetics when he makes a presentation to foundations and/or to individual donors.

I have tried to identify major clusters of activities that occupy much of the time of presidents. Clustering them in this way enables us to interpret the work of the president in educational and theological terms rather than in administrative or management categories. These latter tasks are significant ones as we shall see in the following chapter, but they should be interpreted within the educational framework of the office. Classifying these activities in this way helps make sense out of the multitude of activities in which presidents participate as educators. The classification can also assist in identifying activities which are inappropriate in light of the Gospel and the purpose of the institution.

RECASTING THE WORK

Operating within the educational conceptualization of the office, a president faces tasks with a series of new questions. Who are the students in this situation? What subject matter will we be dealing with? What do we hope to accomplish? How much time do we have? What resources will be needed? Each engagement is faced as an educational opportunity.

A president, working with a board committee, might project a three-year period during which board members would spend a portion of every meeting studying a given subject. The objectives for the study would need to be developed, resources identified, and appropriate periods of time reserved. Could trustees with more knowledge than others share in the teaching? What are the costs of such an educational venture?

In light of difficulties with developing a budget, a member of the executive staff suggests that the group needs to understand the budgeting process better. As moderator of this group, the president assists staff members in identifying what aspect of the budgeting process they wish to comprehend better. Then comes the question of the time and resources needed for dealing with the issue. It may take only an hour; resources may be found within the institution, or brought in from an outside financial planning group.

A president may be invited to spend part of a day with judicatory leaders from the denomination that supports the seminary. The group would like to discuss the offerings of the school in light of clergy needs as they perceive them. The president may ask the group to send her a list of the needs they have identified. Also, what do the judicatory leaders want to happen as a consequence of this meeting? Do they expect the president to change the basic curriculum of the seminary? Do they desire extension classes or continuing education offerings for clergy? Or would they like to know how the seminary's current work is related to the concerns they are raising as active pastors? In focusing such questions, the president is attempting to clarify possible objectives for the session, prepare appropriate resources, and deal with the issues in terms that will make sense to the persons who proposed the meeting. In sum, the president is functioning as an educator.

Whether dealing with plans to strengthen the governing board, or issues which arise in the midst of a staff meeting, or responding to a request from a church group, the president sees each of these situations as opportunities to teach and share in the education of persons concerned with or involved in theological education. Framing these occasions in educational terms provides guidance to the president and casts the activity in a new light.

Having a frame of reference helps, but it does not answer difficult questions for the president. Will we add someone to the development staff or shall we increase the acquisition budget of the library? What will abandoning our residential campus as the primary learning center mean for the type of education we offer? If we offer an extension program, how do we evaluate the adequacy of the education that will take place, even if the program pays for itself? What are the implications of students working alone on their computers to master the content of basic courses? Simply recognizing the educational dimensions to these questions does not afford a president an easy answer. But if the questions are decided without considering the educational implications, a violation of the school's purpose will have occurred.

CONCLUSION

Several persons who read this manuscript as I was working on it raised a variety of questions about the adequacy of the concept of the president as educator. No one highlighted the question, however, that concerns me the most: Where do you find people who know something about education so they can be called to the presidency? In the study done by Mark Holman for this project, he discovered that in recent years more and more presidents have come from the ranks of academic deans. Could this be because a dean knows something of what is involved in the administration of a school, having served as executive officer for a faculty and having worked with a president in the larger administrative duties? We will see how important this is in the next chapter. But deans might also be aware of educational issues in a way that even regular members of the faculty are not. This is especially true because deans commonly have the major responsibility for designing curriculum, or portions of the curriculum. Envisioning educational strategies does not ordinarily occupy the time of faculty members, save for the designing of their own courses. While they may contribute to the curricular discussions, it is usually the dean, and perhaps one or two others, who actually design the learning experience.

I have been a part of a faculty and have watched faculties work on issues for years and am not convinced that faculties always deal with curricular matters in terms of *education*. There are frequently debates over "turf" and personal convenience. How many hours will be given to Old Testament or Church History or Preaching? Do I have to teach a required course? What will this change in the schedule do to my sabbatic plans? If I have to teach during those hours, I will have to do my research when I am less than fresh. These questions and responses are not cast in a manner to encourage educational reflection. In like manner, decisions made by the administration may be made on the basis of convenience rather than education: let's have no changes in the registration after the third day of the term, otherwise the registrar will have to re-do the records; night classes will make the buildings less crowded; we can no longer afford to subsidize the dining room.

Now that I have stated my fears in bold and exaggerated terms, I will confess there are many faculty members who are keenly conscious of educational issues. This is also true of deans and presidents whether they have come from the academy or the parish. Many pastors are sensitive to educational issues and some have taken special training in these areas. There are, in other words, people who are available to become presidents who have both knowledge of and experience in education. Will search committees consider this qualification as being an important one in locating new presidents? Perhaps search committees should hand candidates for the position a copy of the ATS Standards and remind the person that the president is responsible not only for institutional standards (adequate administration, sufficient library and financial resources) but also for the standards for the degrees.

We are fortunate that in our time discussions related to the purpose of theological education have been cast in terms of educational options. The tensions and differences between *paideia* (the process of formation of character) and "Berlin" (symbolizing the research university) and the pragmatic, vocationally-oriented education of much of American higher education have been focal for these debates.[14] There has even been a debate about the nature of education in our popular culture, where terms like virtues, Western civilization, multiculturalism, and the development of the mind have become commonplace.[15] It therefore seems to me that it is possible to find presidents and candidates for the job who consider education vitally important and who have a vision of what good education entails.

For presidents to see themselves as educators is to make possible their discovery of some sense of unity amid the great diversity of activities that fill their personal schedules. But perhaps more important is the fact that a president's constant reminders to the school and the larger community of the institution's educational purpose helps the school find its focal point, its primary goal. The great variety of tasks that each school undertakes— basic degree programs, graduate degrees, continuing education, lay education—are done for some reason. If it is indeed a theological school, what makes it both a school *and* a theological institution is its purpose. Stating clearly and then pursuing an educational purpose brings unity to a school. The president is the leader of this educational process.

NOTES

[1] This definition was developed by Sara Little, Professor Emeritus of Christian Education, and me when we taught together in the 1960s and 1970s at Union Theological Seminary in Virginia. The definition was drawn from our work with Marc Belth, R. S. Peters, and others.

[2] This purpose was developed by David Kelsey in his book *To Understand God Truly*. I am aware that not everyone agrees with Kelsey's statement of the goal of seminary education; readers should therefore substitute their own purpose whenever I use this particular one.

[3] Faculty attitudes toward field education are not consistent. An interesting observation is made by Marjorie Hewitt Suchocki in "Friends in the Family: Church, Seminary, and Theological Education," edited by Joseph C. Hough, Jr. and Barbara G. Wheeler, *Beyond Clericalism: The Congregation as a Focus for Theological Education* (Atlanta: Scholars Press, 1988).

> "Consider also another comparison between medical schools and theological schools. Both require their students to undergo a form of internship: the residency in medicine and field education and/or internship in theological education. The residency appears to be highly valued by the medical profession and is in no sense regarded as inferior to the class work required of the fledgling physician. Rather, the class work seems to culminate in the residency. The field education, however, occupies no similarly elevated place in seminary curricula. Indeed, it is often viewed as marginal to the "truly academic" work of the classroom and as an appendage to the student's education, rather than as the culmination or heart of the process. The internship is likewise regarded with less than unmitigated enthusiasm, with some faculty complaining that such internships diminish the student's zest for the more "demanding" studies of the academy. These attitudes are odd, as we are seeking to provide leadership in the church." 53.

[4] You may note that I did not include attendance at a worship service in the school's chapel among the designed learning experiences. Chapel services are designed for the worship of God, not for educational purposes. Certainly persons learn something by attending worship; they are educated, but that is not the intent of the service. By contrast, a class in liturgics may incorporate a time of prayer or a song of praise, but that is not the same as the gathering of the people of God for worship and praise. Worship and education may indeed overlap, but their purposes should be seen as discrete.

[5] Kelsey, *To Understand God Truly*, 164-5.

[6] Ibid., 118.

[7] Ibid., 164.

[8] Ibid., 164.

[9] Ibid., 121.

[10] Thomas F. Green, *The Activities of Teaching* (New York: McGraw-Hill, 1971), 4-5.

[11] Green's exact definition appears on page 103 of his book. This is a simplified version developed by Sara Little and myself.

[12] Peter M. Senge, *The Fifth Discipline: The Art and Practice of the Learning Organization* (New York: Doubleday/Currency, 1990). Senge believes we can structure organizations

to enable them to become a "learning organization", i.e., one in which persons are encouraged to keep on learning and where the structures help this happen. Learning organizations are "organizations where people continually expand their capacity to create the results they truly desire, where new and expansive patterns of thinking are nurtured, where collective aspiration is set free and where people are continually learning how to learn together." 3.

[13] Max L. Stackhouse,*Apologia: Contextualization, Globalization, and Mission in Theological Education* (Grand Rapids: Eerdmans, 1988).

[14] David H. Kelsey, *Between Athens and Berlin: The Theological Education Debate,* is probably the best example.

[15] George Marsden, for example, traces the history of the decline of the Protestant faith in the life of the university in the USA, *The Soul of the American University:From Protestant Establishment to Established Nonbelief*(New York: Oxford University Press,1994). Douglas Sloan studies the epistemological roots of the exclusion of faith, theology, and the arts from scholarly consideration in contemporary higher education, *Faith and Knowledge: Mainline Protestantism and American Higher Education* (Louisville: Westminster/John Knox Press, 1994). Popular discussions of education are found in such books as Allan David Bloom, *The Closing of the American Mind* (New York: Simon and Schuster, 1987) and William J. Bennett, editor, *The Book of Virtues: A Treasury of Great Moral Stories* (New York: Simon and Schuster, 1993).

5

EDUCATIONAL LEADERSHIP

If we recognize the president as an educator, we must examine how that educator/president leads an institution. A president is expected to be a leader; he is "in charge of" an institution. By definition, CEOs are leaders in our society. But how a president is to lead is not altogether clear nor, for that matter, is the meaning of the word *leadership*. We need to explore what we mean by leadership before relating this to the presidential leadership of an educational institution.

The question of leadership in educational institutions in our time is unclear. Authors of any number of current treatises on presidents in higher education lament the fact that persons occupying the office today do not lead. The overtones of these complaints imply that presidents lack the "guts" or "backbone" to lead as folk did in earlier times.[1] Robert Birnbaum, in his recent book on the presidency in higher education, notes this theme:

> (T)he plaintive query, Where have all the great leaders of the past gone? has an elementary answer: They are dead, along with the simpler times in which formal leaders could wield unbridled power to get what they wanted.[2]

Others, however, do not blame the lack of leadership on the character or constitution of persons currently holding office. They believe the problem lies in the nature of the institution one is supposed to lead. What is it about these institutions that complicates the task of leading? A host of reasons is given. For example, the goals of higher education are not clear and measurable; therefore leaders cannot give direction with clarity nor can progress be measured. Furthermore, it is said that faculty members receive their primary rewards from the academic guilds, not the educational institutions in which they are employed; thus the president has no "leverage" over the "employees." In addition, some say that members of faculty do not value administration and are therefore "casual" toward their own responsibilities of governance. And on and on it goes.[3] Whether one blames the persons in office, the nature of the institution, or the form of governance, the question of leadership is constantly raised.

If the matter is unclear in secular institutions, it is compounded in theological schools, where the lack of clarity about leadership in the churches seeps into the seminary. In many ecclesial settings leaders are viewed as "enablers," persons who stress the process of helping the group or congregation find its own goals and direction. Others have adopted the role of counselor, using patterns derived from the therapeutic arena. But there are also those who believe that only males should be leaders, and that they should give directions with clarity. They try to be—or *their congregations want them to be*—strong, authoritarian leaders. Others reflect the hierarchical tradition of their church organization in which the word of the superior is to be carried out regardless. Leadership is circumscribed by directives from "on high."

In short, there is no *one* view of leadership among churches. Each tradition has a perspective on the subject, an ethos, unspoken assumptions, and ever changing patterns.[4] In honesty, most traditions have several, frequently conflicting, perspectives on the subject which are simultaneously operative in the church.

Added to the studies of leadership in higher education which draw from the worlds of business, military, the human potential movement, and the like, we have another layer which is not entirely separate from the first, but is based on theological and traditional sources which have deep roots in the theological community. It is no wonder the question of presidential leadership is an important one for persons concerned about theological seminaries.

SHARED GOVERNANCE

The context in which one exercises leadership is a significant matter. Leading a small business where most employees are family members is not like leading a major corporation. Leading almost any kind of business differs from leading a not-for-profit organization. But leading some non-profit institutions, e.g. governmental organizations, is different from leading an educational institution. Aaron Wildavsky suggests that leadership is defined by the regime or culture of which it is a part. The shared values of a culture justify leadership practices.[5] Therefore, before we seek to define leadership, let us briefly examine the regime, the form of governance, in which educator/presidents are expected to lead.

The primary issue here has to do with the unique structure of academic governance which many believe contributes to the difficulties of anyone who would be a leader in such institutions. The phrase *shared governance* has been used from time to time in these chapters; we must now examine it more carefully to understand why its structures make leadership difficult. Our discussion will seek neither to praise or blame shared governance, but rather to explicate the task of leadership in terms of the form of governance that currently exists in the majority of educational institutions, including theological ones.

As the phrase implies, the task of governing or leading an educational institution is *shared*. Historically, governing boards have had the legal authority and responsibility for their schools. The trustees or governing board ordinarily own the institution and are responsible for establishing its basic purpose and setting policies for the accomplishment of that purpose. However, to formulate the purpose of an educational institution in our time without dialogue among the various constituencies is risky. Though trustees have the final word on the matter, common sense suggests the wisdom of bringing others "in on the process," especially faculty members since they are key to carrying out the purpose. Such community involvement is "sharing" the governance.

The trustees also have financial responsibility for the institution, to see that monies are raised, well invested and wisely spent. They "share" this work with the administration and occasionally denominational bodies. Boards also may share their responsibility for protecting the good name of the school and advocating on its behalf with these same church instrumentalities.

Board configurations vary: Catholic schools may have a two-tier board[6]; Canadian schools may have a senate in addition to a board; and university-related divinity schools often have no boards save the university one. But where a governing board exists, the president's job is to share with that board in preserving and renewing the school's purpose, in the developing and implementating policies, and in providing the necessary information to ensure that adequate policies and plans are established.

The "sharing" that is our focus, however, is that which involves the faculty, whose participation became prominent during the late 1950s and early 1960s. A document titled "Joint Statement on Government of Colleges and Universities" was issued in 1966 by the American Association of University Professors (AAUP). It affirms there is an inescapable interdependence among the governing board, administration, and faculty. This document assumes there will be adequate communication among these groups and appropriate opportunities for joint planning. It suggests that in certain important matters, all of the groups should have a voice. While addressing other constituencies, the AAUP was and is primarily concerned with faculty involvement in governance. Birnbaum notes this development:

> As institutions became more comprehensive and involved in scholarship, the faculty became more specialized, more professionalized, and less tolerant of administrative controls. Increasingly until World War II, and then with accelerating force during the 1950s and 1960s, faculty claimed for themselves not only the right to make decisions concerning the major educational activities of the institution, but also to participate fully in setting institutional policy and to have a voice in its management. The growing power of the faculty, a change significant enough to justify referring to it as the "academic revolution," was one of the forces that led postwar presidents to claim that "the fundamental difficulty with the office of university president arises out of the current system of controlling modern universities...He has vast responsibilities for all phases of the life and welfare of the university, but he has no power."[7]

In their classic study based on research done in the late 1960s and early 1970s, Cohen and March concluded that educational institutions should be thought of as "organized chaos" because of the practice of shared governance. The decision-making processes had become so complex and dysfunctional that they were referred to as "the garbage can theory of decision making."[8] A few years later, William R. Brown traced the mindset or culture of faculty that makes its participation in governance problematic.[9] In fact, he argues, faculty concerns are frequently antithetical to those of organization and administration.

But to state the case positively, the faculty shares in the governance of a school with the president and board by establishing admission policies, calling new faculty members, designing curricula, evaluating student performance, and recommending persons for degrees to the trustees; and in some cases, it is given considerable responsibility for the common life, such as worship, overseeing student government, and community functions. Faculty members are ordinarily jealous of their prerogatives in setting these policies and managing their own academic lives. For example, a recommendation for tenure or promotion sent to the board by the faculty must have very serious questions before the board dares reverse the faculty's decision. In cases where the board has overturned a decision on such matters, deep divisions have been created and a state of low morale engendered.

Many policies set by the board impinge on faculty life, such as the question of sabbatic leaves, granting of tenure, and academic freedom. Faculty want to be and should be involved through the administration in the formation of these policies. When it is a matter that can be labeled strictly academic, then the faculty share primary, if not quite sole, responsibility. But it is clear there are grey areas involved that relate to the board and administration as well as the faculty. In all of these matters, clear and unclear, the president is held accountable by the board for the academic program and policies of the institution even though it is the faculty that determines these matters.

Student involvement in governance became an issue in the late 1960s and early 1970s. There is now often a student trustee. At times, students are asked to serve on faculty committees and even on trustee committees. These persons are frequently given a vote; in other situations they are only given "voice." One way or the other, their presence is an effort to encourage communication and allow them to share in forming institutional policy. There currently is concern for nonacademic staff such as secretaries, building and grounds supervisors, dieticians, and others to share in the processes of governance. What shape or form this will take is not yet clear.

How does the president fit into this scheme? As we have seen, some think "poorly" is the appropriate answer. The AAUP document mentioned before speaks of the president's responsibilities for *sharing* in defining and attaining goals, for communication within and without the institution, and as the chief planner. It also noted that the chief executive officer may have to intervene in certain faculty matters, usually having to do with the removal of a faculty member.

Leadership in governing an institution with all of these parties sharing in decision making is complex. An educational institution is unlike any other institution. The leadership needed to move such a convoluted governance apparatus in even a small school is unique and difficult. In this setting the leadership role is viewed from many different perspectives; the same president can be accused simultaneously of not offering aggressive leadership and of acting like a dictator. And, as is the case whenever one discusses theological schools, these institutions vary greatly with respect to the degree of shared governance that the ethos of the school and the tradition dictate. A special form of leadership must be exercised in a shared fashion even in institutions that belong to religious traditions which are accustomed to decisions being made from the top down.

It should be noted at this point, for it will be expanded upon later, that the president is uniquely situated in the shared governance arrangement. She is the only one who relates to every segment of the community and its constituencies. She has some type of relationship with faculty, staff, students, trustees, donor groups, church associations, and local civic community leaders. It is this location in the complex that enables her to exercise leadership. It is also this location that causes everyone to expect the president to "handle" or "manage" difficult situations even though the structure may not grant her the authority needed to make the decisions.

LEADERSHIP

In light of the realities of shared governance, a presidential search committee might well wonder how the *leader* they are looking for will behave. When a presidential evaluation committee says it expects more *leadership*, what do they want to see the president do? To suggest that a seminary president should exercise leadership is almost like saying: "Do something. We're not sure what, nor do we know how one does it, but for heaven's sake do something!"

One way to approach the issue is to use a carefully crafted definition of leadership to throw light on the subject. Individuals, traditions, and institutions will each want to add their own cast to the product, but for the purposes of this discussion, I have selected the work of Joseph Rost who is uniquely helpful in addressing the questions of leadership in higher education.[10]

Rost offers a definition of leadership he believes will be useful to the practitioner as well as the scholar/researcher. Like most of us, he is troubled by the fact that when one reads books on leadership, one is told that leadership involves remembering the history of the organization, or, that leaders motivate others, or, that leadership embodies the values of the institution, or, that leaders define reality, or, that leadership means bringing changes. Clearly, leaders do all of these things at different times and under varying circumstances. But what is leadership?

Rost argues for a definition of leadership that is clear, concise, understandable by scholars and practitioners, and that is researchable, practically relevant, and persuasive.[11] He proposes the following:

Leadership is an influence relationship among leaders and followers who intend real changes that reflect their mutual purposes.[12]

In this definition, leadership is a *relationship*, a relationship based on *influence*.[13] In such a relationship, influence flows back and forth among the parties involved, but the influence behaviors must not be coercive. Many other types of "influencing" are available, e.g., persuasion based on personality, the content of one's teaching, reputation or prestige, even "location" in the institution. Persons involved in this relationship are free to agree or disagree with one another. There is no pressure "from the top down" in the sense of authoritarian demands.

In any such relationship, there are leaders and followers, though the latter word should not be interpreted as implying *passive followers*. Followers are actively involved in the leadership relationship. In the midst of the discussion, the leader —a president, for example—may become a follower as he hears a point of view that alters his position; he follows someone else's lead. He may again become the leader as he integrates this new insight into his proposal and presents his case in light of this new information. He is weighing the evidence, making judgments; he is the "student" in a teaching situation, though he may again become the teacher as the process goes on.

We are not talking about a one-on-one type of relationship; we are referring to situations where there are several followers. Rost suggests that one-on-one relationships build friendship and thus may be supportive and helpful in some way at a later point when the president is leading. This earlier one-on-one relationship may add to his influence, but it is not in itself a leadership relation. In our illustration, we are dealing with a president talking with the faculty. In this example, the president was influenced by a leader among the faculty, a person who knew more about the particular subject than anyone in the room. After further conversation, the president may again become a follower as another leader from the faculty helps the group see yet another important issue. The point is that the relationship is fluid; influence shifts back and forth between active followers and leaders. Because of the overall knowledge of the institution, the president's influence at times will be stronger than that of others; there is thus an inequality in the relationship. At the same time, when a faculty member becomes a leader, the relationship will again be unequal, this time in favor of the faculty member. Depending on the issue, it may be that throughout the conversation the president will have greater influence because of his position and knowledge than the others, though there still will be the shifting of roles.

I want to underscore the parallel between the description of what is going on in a faculty meeting and education. If the president is a good teacher, he will have "designed" the learning process by providing appropriate material for reading before the meeting, and by structuring the conversation so that members of the faculty are asked to decide issues based on the teaching and learning taking place in the meeting. While this is true of faculty meetings, it is also true of trustee meetings where the president is usually responsible for setting the agenda, or, organizing the teaching/learning experience.

In the following scenario, both the president and faculty members intend to bring about a specific change. They *purposefully* desire to alter the admissions process so it will be more inclusive. This would be a *real* change, a significant shift in the life of the school with ramifications for the churches. It would alter the student body and probably have considerable impact on courses offered. They may not be able to agree on a new policy immediately; there may be many meetings and numerous drafts, but leadership is taking place throughout the process. The president and the dean may also be sharing the proposals with the board's committee on academic affairs, since they have the final word. In fact, the governing board may have much more to do with a policy change of this order than this illustration suggests. But to keep the illustration simple, let us assume the president and the faculty are agreed that a change needs to be made, and they are working on it. It is their *intent* to bring about a real or significant *change* that distinguishes the relationship as a leadership one. The impetus for change in this case may have originated with the president, but now the faculty is involved in the process. Or, it might well have originated with the dean. Regardless of the origin, the intent is for faculty to think, know, feel, and decide about the matter of admissions.

As leaders and followers discuss the new policy over a period of months, they may change their minds several times. They may see they need to change portions of the curriculum before they can instigate a new admissions policy. The *intent* of bringing about change that will basically alter the institution is a sign of leadership.

Of course not all change is good; it is possible to propose changes that could be detrimental to the institution. Some leaders instigate changes that lead schools into dreadful situations; their leadership may be disastrous. The changes proposed should always be evaluated in terms of the institution's basic purpose and commitments. Only when change enhances these is the change for the good.

As the president and faculty work on the matter of admissions they are developing *mutual purposes*. These arise out of noncoercive influence relationships; no imposition of a new policy is going to be mandated from a higher authority, although policies of the church and/or other institutions may be examined. No member of the faculty will threaten to resign if such-and-such a policy is adopted. Rather the new policy or, let us say, purpose, is forged in the give and take of leaders and followers. Rost uses the term *purposes* rather than goals because the latter generally refers to steps designed by managers to see that certain things get done. Leadership is involved with larger issues—with changing the institution, not running it. There is an appropriate place for management and its goals, but they are not to be confused with leadership.

Rost would contend that even if circumstances prevented development of a new admissions policy, leadership was taking place nonetheless because the intended change reflected their purpose. One might say their intent has become a common purpose, an expression of the institution's calling.

The notion of an institution having a calling or a vocation may seem strange to us, yet if the leader is able to nurture agreed upon purposes, this is indeed descriptive of what is happening. Robert Lynn observes that

> At the root of the creative institution is a shared sense of vocation or, if you prefer, a common calling. In both the Jewish and Christian traditions, the presence of calling is embraced as a gift. The consequences of that gift are evident in a corporate sense of identity and in a unifying loyalty to a set of purposes. If that root sense of mission either has died or is decaying, the whole institution will sooner or later be affected in every respect. Nothing can be more subtle or serious an ailment than this sort of root disease. But whenever an institution undergoes renewal, its new life often springs from a deepened commitment to its vocation.[14]

Leadership, then, has four essential elements: a relationship based on influence, a relationship involving leaders and followers, who intend real changes, and who develop mutual purposes.[15]

The notion of a leader becoming a follower and then a leader again seems to be contrary to our assumption that the president by virtue of office is a leader. The prior illustration of the faculty meeting was used to underscore, first, that leadership is a relationship and, second, that there are many leaders in most situations. Followers in the seminary community's discussion of admissions may be leaders in their guild; leaders in business may be followers as board members; the president may be a leader in the theological institution but a follower in the financial investing arena.[16] But because of the president's position and the knowledge, responsibilities, and authority that go with it, the president is ordinarily a leader in the theological community.[17]

As we have seen, there is an inherent inequality in the leadership relationship: leaders usually have more influence. This is especially true of presidents. While they may feel from time to time that they have little or no influence, this is not the case. Their location between the board and the institution gives them influence; their control, even limited control, of the budget gives them influence. They probably know more about the school than anyone else; they know what is going on when others know only part of what's happening. Their unique knowledge of the institution gives them influence. If they are good students of institutions and organizations, they know more about how theological schools run than any one else. To use Rost's phrase, these are *power resources* for influencing others that belong primarily to the president.

A president, then, is exercising leadership when she engages in an influence relationship with other persons of the theological community, with the intent to bring about real changes based on the mutually agreed upon purposes of the community.

This definition of leadership meshes with our definitions of education and teaching as well as the realities of the shared governance of most theological institutions. It is through the president's relationships with various constituencies that she is able to *influence* the diverse aspects of the school's life, and to do so uniquely. No one else is related to all of these persons; no one else can design the learning experience for so many different groups. She exercises influence through her educational designs and activities of teaching. In our illustration, the president exercised leadership in the academic realm without in any way denying that the dean and faculty have been given the responsibility of leading the academic programs of the school. The president and the dean also will have to use their influence with the board to educate and enable them to see and buy into the new purpose or policy. There even may be a need to "influence" the staff in the admission's office so they can share fully in the implementation of the new approach. The president is uniquely situated to have this influence on these several bodies, to teach them, to educate them.

If one uses this definition, one must also acknowledge that much of what a president does is not leadership. It is management or administration, depending on how one defines those terms. We have been stressing collegial relationships, but there are relationships of authority; the president, for instance, instructs persons on the staff to prepare for a reception. There are routine matters such as dealing with the questions of auditors and writing notes of appreciation to donors. These are not unimportant matters, but they are not necessarily occasions for the exercise of leadership. John Kotter notes that "strong leadership with weak management is no better, and sometimes actually worse, than the reverse." [18] To realize one does not have to be a leader all the time can be extremely freeing for a president. It means presidents can recognize that much of what they do is administration.

EDUCATIONAL ADMINISTRATION

When a president proposes to the board's committee on buildings and grounds that a five-year maintenance program be developed by the administration, he is assuming a leadership role. This will constitute a major change in the life of the school. There will be plans that can be assigned budget figures, personnel requirements, and deadlines for accepting bids. To have the needs spelled out for five years constitutes a significant step in the overall planning process. It will take some educating of both the board committee and the staff to bring this off, but it is a change sorely needed.

Two years later, when the president works with the business manager to bring before the board committee an update of the five- year plan, the president is functioning as an administrator. When the president directs the maintenance crew to prepare a certain room for faculty meetings every fourth Thursday, he is engaged in management. Since the faculty has agreed to hold their monthly meeting on that day, the president is implementing this agreement upon policy.

Admittedly, these terms—leadership, administration, and management—are not defined by all in the same way, nor are the lines separating the activities always as clear as my illustrations might imply.

But for practical purposes, this is one way to analyze the work of the president.

We have looked briefly at what it means for an educator to lead and now need to relate that conversation to the task of *administration*. To administer is to manage or supervise the execution of policies, the use of resources, and the conduct of the operation of an institution. At its heart, the word *administer* deals with ministry, serving. It is the service a president renders to the community by keeping the institution faithful to its agreed upon purposes. Does the budget reflect the stated purposes? The same question should be asked about the use of space and resources. Does the common life of the institution move along with some sense of order and orderliness so the various groups—faculty, staff, students—can do what they are called to do? Are there administrative policies—guidelines for keeping these matters on course—in place and are they being followed and reviewed periodically?

While the word *administration* is associated with business organizations in the minds of most persons, the word has biblical roots as well as an ecclesiastical tradition. The linguistic origin of the word *administration* as used in 1 Corinthians 12, which refers to the *gift of administration*, is that of steering a ship. As the one who steers the ship is under orders from the captain, so the latter is working under orders from the owner.[19] Or, the captain is one who works in partnership with God, fellow human beings, and nature. As the captain encourages, supports, and enables each member of the crew to use their particular gifts for the sake of operating the vessel, so a president as administrator, assists, encourages, and supports members of the seminary community as they work together to provide an educational experience for the sake of the ministry of the church.[20] Simply having an agreed upon purpose does not make these things happen automatically anymore than having a destination for a ship guarantees the vessel will stay on course and arrive. Someone must see that the pilot is at the wheel and knowledgeable about the course, that the sailors in the galley know when to serve meals so the rest of the crew can eat, that the living quarters are cleaned, the cargo checked, and a host of other things. The captain is seeing to all of these things. By his efforts and instructions, others are able to use their gifts and talents in fulfilling the mission.

Thomas Campbell and Gary Reierson underscore the importance of administration as ministry:

... ministry occurs *in* and through administration. This is different from saying that administration *serves* ministry or that administrative insights may be used to *manage* ministry. Until the ordained clergy [and academics] recognize that administration is a central locus *of* ministry and *is* itself ministry, there will be no central motivation, either for them or for others within the community of believers, to exercise administrative functions with sensitivity and joy.[21]

But as indicated in the opening of this section, the president also engages in management. If the president has a well-qualified staff, he may delegate much of the management of the institution to these persons. The Vice President for Academic Affairs *manages* the policies set by the faculty for limits on enrollment, due dates for theses, sequencing of courses, and the like. The same officer is also an administrator who guides the faculty in the development of a new curriculum, who initiates a new program to fulfill the school's purposes. The Business Manager manages the payroll, the payment of bills by students in accordance with institutional policies, and exercises administrative oversight of the dining room and parking lot. The Vice President for Development, or Institutional Advancement, administers the operations of this area by making sure that alumni/ae records are up to date, that donors are sent letters of appreciation, and other such management functions.

As the president works with an executive staff, usually four or five persons, she may indeed be exercising leadership in developing a new organizational approach or restructuring some existing area of the school's life. She becomes a follower when the dean or academic vice president proposes a new way for students to be involved with congregations. She may engage in management as the group sets up a special meeting for friends of the seminary. A president should be able to move smoothly among these functions without always imagining herself to be a leader. She can learn to administer and manage with both skill and joy. Presidents are "servant leaders."[22]

TEAM LEADERSHIP

Because of the tremendous number of duties and expectations placed upon a president, and because of the nature of shared governance, leadership in educational institutions might well be described as team leadership. The president and the board make a team; the president and faculty are a team; the president and staff are yet another team. Most institutions, even fairly small ones, have some type of administrative staff or executive staff—a small group that works directly with the president. Bolman and Deal note in their *Modern Approaches to Understanding and Managing Organizations* that one can coordinate and control an organization through authority and rules *vertically*, but one can also coordinate and lead an organization *laterally* through the use of meetings, committees, and task forces.[23] There is a sense in which the latter is more congenial to the concept of shared governance, though one suspects there is always a little of both in every system. It also means that presidents need to learn to work with teams of active followers/leaders

There are a number of teams in any institution, but this section will focus on the small group of staff members who work directly with the president in the administration of the institution. In many cases, some of these people will be faculty members who serve as administrators part time. In one university divinity school, five people, the entire staff, are faculty members with additional responsibilities. In almost all institutions, the academic vice president has faculty status. More and more, however, even small theological schools are finding it necessary and advantageous to employ full-time administrators to work with the president, with the exception of the dean, chief academic officer. Whenever this opportunity arises, a president should employ the most experienced and best-equipped administrator he can find; he should never fear being "overshadowed" by a member of the staff. Good staff members only increase the effectiveness of the CEO.

Estela Bensimon and Anna Neumann have produced a very good guide titled *Redesigning Collegiate Leadership: Teams and Teamwork in Higher Education*.[24] They envision that the president will lead the institution primarily through his work with an administrative team. They point out the advantage of having several persons addressing a problem or issue. When a staff is composed of persons representing academic, fiscal, and development concerns, along with concerns of students—with the president representing concerns of trustees and outside constituencies—the result is that each problem and issue is viewed from different angles and interests. There are more skills, perspectives, and information available in such a group than any one person alone could embody; thus the solutions or proposals are more likely to be creative and constructive for the whole community, not for just one segment. The very fact that different areas of the school's life are in communication with one another clearly has advantages. When a decision is reached, staff share responsibility for interpreting the action to various segments of the community and gaining support for the decision.

Some decisions belong to the Academic Dean and some to the Vice President for Administration or the Dean of Students. But if these persons discuss thoroughly the issue before them, they not only receive feedback from the viewpoints of others, but also build support for the decision they must make. And a most important rule is being followed: the president will not be surprised by the decision of a member of the staff. It is a healthy situation when staff members learn from one another in the process of making key decisions for the institution.

There is always a danger that staff will become isolated from the rest of the community. Some observers of educational institutions note that administrators find talking to one another comfortable since they share a common frame of reference and sense of collegiality in their work. Usually administrative offices are close together and the necessity of daily work calls upon these folk to communicate. It is therefore extremely important for the president and administrative staff to stay in close contact with other members of the community. The president needs to make special efforts to visit with faculty and staff. At the same time, faculty members should make special efforts to share with the president matters that concern them. Again, it may be part of the president's educational task to encourage both faculty and staff to keep communication open in all directions.

It always takes more time to work with a team than it does to do it on your own, but the leadership team is well worth the time and extra effort. Bensimon and Neumann offer concrete help in learning to work productively as a team. From the perspective of this book, one might say the leadership staff is one of the best opportunities the president has to serve as an educator who teaches. The teaching and learning done in this group permeates the entire institution. The history, vision, and values of the school need to be learned and relearned again and again. Such a leadership team can become a jazz combo, making beautiful music.[25]

The numbers of things presidents are responsibile for, dirfectly or indirectly, is such that exercising leadership through and with a team may be one of the only ways a president can survive in a seminary, even a small one. Having an assistant to the president may help with many details, but ordinarily these persons do not have the status of an executive staff member. Trustees interested in making the president's life and longevity in office possible need to consider the benefits as well as the costs of a team to work with the president.

BACK TO REALITY

I believe the interpretation of the president as an educator can be useful to the president and the theological community. It enables both to view the position in a more constructive way. It provides a framework for understanding how leadership can be exercised in the educational community and the place of administration as a form of service in that community. With the assistance of a good team, theological schools can be led and administered in a fashion that is educative.

Having said all of that, I must acknowledge that the preceding discussion omits a number of important matters. For example, the illustrations used suggest that the president and the dean, or the president and the faculty, or the president and the board, are "in tune" with one another on such things as new admission policies; thus the development of new approaches is merely a matter of "influencing" one another until the desired change is accomplished. In fact, there are faculty members who oppose any change, especially one suggested by the president. And there are presidents who never think about proposing a change since all they intend to do is keep the doors open until they can retire or be reassigned. Some boards have little good to say about the faculty and there are faculties which ignore the board in so far as possible. There can be jealousy and competition within an executive staff—between the chief academic officer and the president, for example. In other words, things do not flow along simply; influence is often rejected; finding a mutually agreed upon purpose can be very, very difficult and time consuming. Such realities do not deny the thesis of these chapters, but indicate that the task is not as easy as the writing may imply.

A second matter, related to the above and only alluded to in passing, has to do with the deeply ingrained antipathy felt by some academicians toward administration and management. If one's colleagues do not respect the work being done, it is bound to affect the person doing the work. A president writing his memoirs as a part of this project recorded this exchange:

> As I was finishing the first draft of this essay, I was approached by a friend who inquired what I was doing. "Oh," he said, "are you writing that book on Christian ethics I've been waiting for?"

"No," I replied, "it is a project on what it means to be a seminary
president."

"Oh," he responded,"too bad."

Such an attitude can dampen anyone's efforts, even those intending to serve
God.[26] One way a president can deal with this reality is to become a teacher
to the rest of the community. It would be interesting to see if some faculty
leaders would read and discuss with the president a book like the one by
William Brown, *Academic Politics*, which deals with faculty culture and
participation in governance.

But all of the learning is not to come from one side. Faculty can
frequently point out areas in which administrative procedures are distorting
the educational purposes of the institution. Being a part of these procedures
can blind even the most sensitive of presidents. Such critiquing of the
leadership, administration, and management of the institution is important,
otherwise the interests of administrators and managers become primary
rather than serving the educational purposes of the school. Such give and
take within the community is healing and creative for all concerned.
Leadership is greatly needed at this point in the academic community.

A third item that has been neglected is the type of change leaders
work to bring about. The only qualifier we have mentioned is that change
must be for the good of the institution. As indicated, much of the literature
dealing with leadership points to particular changes the authors believe
constitute either leadership or signs of the same. My belief is that in light of
her understanding of the Gospel, the nature of ministry, and the calling of
the institution, each president has to decide what that "good" is that now
demands her best efforts, time, and influence.

A president cannot change everything. A president must be selective
in undertaking major changes in the life and structure of a school. There
may be smaller things that need changing in the institution, but these must
be left to others, while she identifies key issues that will not be faced unless
she as president brings them before the community. My illustration of
changing the admission policy may be misleading at this point. While this
could be a significant change for some schools, I would assume that the
president would ordinarily work with the dean or chief academic officer
and leave the major leadership in such cases to that person. But after
identifying the changes the president believes she must assume
responsibility for, she then is faced with the educational task of enabling
others to join her in the effort.

CONCLUSION

Much of what has been said in this and the preceding chapter may appear contrary to the ideas our society holds about "presidents" and "leaders." Presidents of seminaries may not be as highly respected as we remember earlier presidents being, but without question they still are respected and given certain privileges within their own communities and in the larger arena.[27] That a president would be at times a follower rather than a leader is not generally assumed. As the chief administrator of an institution, few staff members think of him as serving; instead, they see themselves as serving him. That a president would spend time in management rather than leadership is a demeaning idea to some. That presidents share the leadership functions with others does not seem to fit our image any more than seeing the president as an educator by the way he works with the community.

In 1900 John Knox McLean argued that presidents should no longer be primarily teachers but *executives*, persons who execute policies, get things done, find resources. Leadership during that era was conceived primarily in terms of *power*. My contention near the end of the century is that presidents do function as executives; they do get things done. But they do so by exercising *influence*, by being the servant leaders, the ones who design processes that enable people to think, know, feel, and decide about the serious matter of theological education. They lead by teaching, by reasoning, by drawing out implications, by pointing to consequences, by witnessing to the truth. They lead by their passion and persuasion on behalf of the education of church leaders, by their vision of the mission of God's people in our time.

I am inclined to think the notion of the president as educator/teacher, one who leads by influencing others, is congenial with the biblical words about serving and also provides a basis for ongoing realistic, self-evaluation in situations where presidents are granted honor and prestige.

NOTES

[1] We read, for example, in the publication *Integrity in the College Curriculum*: "Their [this generation of academic presidents] visions must be bolder, their initiatives more energetic and imaginative, and the great potential for academic leadership that is latent in the authority of their positions must be asserted forcefully and skillfully." Estela M. Bensimon,"The Meaning of Presidential Leadership: Alternative to Charismatic Approaches," in *Women at the Helm*, edited by Sturnick, Milley and Tisinger (Washington, D. C.: American Association of State Colleges and Universities, 1991), 74. The quotation is from the publication named (Washington,D. C.: Association of American Colleges, 1985).

[2] Robert Birnbaum, *How Academic Leadership Works: Understanding Success and Failure in the College Presidency*(San Francisco: Jossey-Bass 1992), xii.

[3] Madeleine Green, "Investing In Leadership", *Liberal Education*,vol.76,no.1,(Jan.-Feb.,1990), 6-13. William R. Brown, *Academic Politics*(University, Ala.: The University of Alabama Press, 1982). For authors who focus particularly on the nature of the institution, see Michael D. Cohen and James G. March,*Leadership and Ambiguity: The American College President* (Boston: Harvard Business School Press, Second Edition, 1986) and James G. March and Johan P. Olsen, *Ambiguity and Choice in Organizations* (Bergen: Universitetsforlaget, second edition, 1979.)

[4] See Jackson W.Carroll, *As One with Authority: Reflective Leadership in Ministry* (Louisville: Westminster/John Knox Press,1991), for a discussion of a portion of this issue.

[5] Aaron Wildavsky, *The Nursing Father: Moses as a Political Leader* (The University of Alabama Press, 1984), 182ff.

[6] Katarina Schuth, an authority on Catholic seminary education notes: " A common understanding about what should be the role of boards of trustees does not exist. Some function mainly for promotion and fund-raising purposes, while others are policy-making. Because of the brief history of diverse membership in the governance of Roman Catholic institutions, it will take some time to evolve new patterns." *Reason for the Hope:The Futures of Roman Catholic Theologates* (Wilmington: Michael Glazier, Inc.,1989), 62.

[7] Robert Birnbaum," The College Presidency: An Impossible Job", 32-33 in John C. Smart, editor, *Higher Education: Handbook of Theory and Research*, vol.5 (New York: Agathon Press, 1989). The reference to "academic revolution" refers to C. Jenks and D. Riesman, *The Academic Revolution* (1968) and the quotation is from H. P. Rainey: "How shall we control our universities? Why college presidents leave their jobs," in *Journal of Higher Education*,31:376-383, no specific page given.

[8] Michael D. Cohen and James G. March, *Leadership and Ambiguity*, Second Edition,(Boston: Harvard Business School Press, 1984.)

[9] William R. Brown, *Academic Politics* (University, Alabama: The University of Alabama Press, 1982).

[10] Joseph C. Rost. *Leadership for the Twenty-First Century*. New York: Praeger, 1991.

[11] Joseph Rost, op. cit., 99.

[12] Ibid., 102. John P.Kotter, *A Force for Change: How Leadership Differs from Management* (New York: The Free Press,1990), 3, suggests that *leadership* can be used as a process or as a noun. Both he and Professor Rost are clearly using the word as a process.

[13] I personally am ambiguous about using this definition. The writings of Max Depree and others are in some way much more satisfying to read. Yet when one finishes those articles or books, one has no real definition of leadership at hand. Leadership is some capacity to "make room for families," "to have ideas," "to listen," "leaders tell the companies stories," "they are able to define reality," etc. There seems to be no single agreed upon capacity, but whatever the writer saw as necessary at the time. I therefore use Rost's definition because it avoids these other pitfalls, though it lacks the sense of substance one finds in an article like Donald Shriver's "Visions and Nightmares: The Leader's Call to See Reality—and Change It"(*In Trust*, New Year, 1992), 16-20.

[14] Robert Lynn, an editorial in the Annual Report of the Lilly Endowment,Inc., for 1984 on "Penetrating the Mystery of Leadership," 8.

[15] Ibid., 104.

[16] Ibid., 109.

[17] John Kotter, another writer in the field of leadership, agrees with this when he affirms that any organization has many leaders throughout the system. There are leaders in the governing board; there are leaders in the faculty, among the staff and in the student body. Hopefully, all of these leaders are held together by what Kotter calls "thick informal networks," especially a common commitment to the purposes of the school.See *A Force for Change: How Leadership Differs from Management,* 31, 89ff.

[18] John Kotter, op. cit., p.17. Joseph F.Kaufman, in his book, *At the Pleasure of the Board: The Service of the College and University President* (Washington, D. C.: The American Council on Education, 1980), suggests that a president should first be a leader; that is, leadership has a priority. But he suggests that other roles include the representational, the role of communicator and interpreter, and finally that of management and control. 13-14.

[19] *Theological Dictionary of the New Testament*, edited by Gerhard Kittel, translator and editor, Geoffrey W. Bromiley, Vol. III (Grand Rapids: Eerdmans, 1965). The noun form of the verb, to steer a ship, thus refers to the "helmsman" as is seen in Acts 27:11 and Rev. 18:17. The figure is used for a statesman at times in secular writings:"steering" and the "art of the helmsman." There is also reference in other literature to divine helmsman or the governance of God. See 1035.

[20] Thomas C. Campbell and Gary B. Reierson,*The Gift of Administration: Theological Bases for Ministry* (Philadelphia: The Westminster Press, 1981), 36ff.

[21] Op. cit., 106.

[22] The reference here is to the work of Robert K. Greenleaf cited in the notes of Chapter One.

[23] Lee G. Bolman and Terrence E. Deal, *Modern Approaches to Understanding and Managing Organizations* (San Francisco: Jossey-Bass, 1989), 41.

[24] Estela Bensimon and Anna Neumann, *Redesigning Collegiate Leadership: Team and Teamwork in Higher Education* (Baltimore: The Johns Hopkins University Press, 1993.) While acknowledging that this is a very useful book, I would add that it is like many research projects; it looks at only one piece, focuses on that, and neglects the context in which the team, in this case, works. The ideas and practical suggestions are nevertheless helpful.

[25] I have used this illustration for years, but was delighted to read Max DePree's recent *Leadership Jazz* (New York: Doubleday, 1992) which confirms my belief in the analogy.

[26] Other illustrations of the attitude are abundant. For example, Madeleine Green writes

...the culture of higher education dictates that administration, or management, is a necessary evil, supporting however clumsily the true center of a college or university—teaching and learning. Administration, in short, is not a very lofty art. Often we hear of the administrator who took the job under duress, intending to return to the classroom at the first available opportunity. The true member of the academic community is expected to long for the classroom and the library. Management connotes the mundane, the operational, the ability to get things done toward the accomplishment of a predetermined goal. Leadership, on the other hand, provides shape, direction, and meaning, and is therefore far more intellectually respectable.Madeleine F. Green,ed. *Leaders for a New Era: Strategies for Higher Education (New York: Macmillan, 1988), 16.*

Even more interesting is the comment of Patricia R. Plante:

In sum, in the academy, when discussing those who profess and those who administer, two unquestioned premises often obtain. Those who choose to devote their professional lives to teaching and research did so for motives that transcend the self. Those who decided to spend their careers engaged in management, broadly defined so as to include leadership, did so for reasons that center on the self. Hence, one is able to trust the first group, but must be wary of the second. Patricia R. Plante with Robert L. Caret, *Myths and Realities of Academic Administration* (New York: Macmillan, 1990), 57.

[27] The study done for this project by Wade Clark Roof on the views of denominational leaders—both lay and clergy—toward seminary presidents indicate that in most traditions, seminary presidents are still valued and recognized as leaders to some extent. The recognition and honor is greater among the more conservative denominations.

6

THE PRESIDENT AS PERSON

As Clark Kerr and Marian Gade remind us:

The floating factor in each type of situation is the president—his or her strategies and tactics, skills and character. The interaction of environments and character constitute a great continuing drama played out on many stages before many audiences.[1]

It is the personality, gifts and interest, previous experience and training, faith and dreams which an individual brings to the office that contributes more than any other single factor to the shaping of a presidency. But, as Kerr and Gade observe, it is the interaction of this person with a particular environment that constitutes the continuing drama of the presidency.

I know of no way to describe how each person's uniqueness is going to contribute to a particular office since the schools themselves are constantly passing through different phases in their life cycles, and the sociocultural environment is always in flux. There is no way to project in the abstract the impact this or that person will have on the presidency of an institution, nor is there a way to envision the environmental changes that may take place while a person is president. While a carefully executed search process can prevent institutions from making horrendous mistakes, there is no way to forecast with one hundred percent accuracy the effectiveness of a person in the office based on the committee's perception of the person's gifts, experience, and vision. No one really knows the conditions that will come to bear upon the presidency in the next five years.

What we can do, however, is reflect on the person of the president which intersects the institutional environment at crucial points. My purpose in this chapter, therefore, will be to discuss personal aspects of the presidency, such as the calling to the office, the support a person needs while in the office, and how the president thinks about leaving—which is of concern to both the president and the institution. The drama of the presidency is played out in the interaction of the president and the institution. That is before us in these pages.

THE CALL

We begin our discussion with some thoughts on the call a president receives. The search process which leads to a call is critically important. It is so important that a special study was conducted by Mark A. Holman as part of this project. The study has been published and I will not attempt to repeat his helpful insights here. His book has been widely used and must be considered required reading for search committees.[2] I am assuming Holman's research and writing will be investigated by concerned parties, and therefore will focus this discussion on the sense of calling which a candidate experiences and its match or "fit" with the community of faith to which that person is being called. Search committees need to reflect on this matter as much as candidates, for they must interact with each other or there will be no call.

In many professions there are fairly clear career moves one follows to become a success, to reach the top, to become CEO. Even within university settings, it is possible to trace a career pattern of sorts, though few people set out to become university presidents. But the situation with theological schools is ordinarily quite different.

In the memoirs of the presidents who wrote for this project, there was no mention of career move, but rather words about "being called" or "of having a sense of calling to the office." I do not think these people were suggesting they alone have such calls or that callings and career tracks are antithetical. I believe their language underscores their awareness that they were taking a position because of a conviction that God was somehow involved in their selection. I do not take this as merely pious rhetoric to cover personal ambitions. Some will acknowledge they wanted the position; they are not ashamed of this. Others do not openly say this but will acknowledge the same if asked. The underlying theme is simply an awareness of God's call to serve in this place at this time. Many ecclesial traditions refer to this as *an internal call of God*.

But the call comes in quite different ways. It comes to some folk through the community. This is especially true of internal candidates, faculty members or board members—persons who have had considerable contact with the school over a period of time. Frequently these persons have participated in a relocation study, a critical reorganization study, or some other significant committee assignment. Such groups are usually made up of trustees, faculty, students, and graduates. The group arrives at a reasonably clear picture of what the school is faced with in the days ahead. Later, when the search committee turns to a member of this group and says, "You are what we need at this time in the life of the school," it can be read as a call. Because the people involved are knowledgeable of both the institution and the individual, the latter must take the call seriously. One can refer to this as *a community call*.

Closely akin to this is the *obedience call*. This is part of the Roman Catholic tradition, though it also is experienced by others. The superior of the order or the bishop, after consultation and frequently a search process, will approach a member of the community or order with the call to become rector of their seminary. One accepts the calling as part of obedience, even though one may not have sought such a position. The candidate realizes he possess the gifts and probably can do the job; at times he even may be eager and excited about the work.

Many deans of university divinity schools come to their positions in a similar fashion. The search is frequently an internal one; that is, selecting one of the colleagues to serve as dean for a season. The person accepts the calling as part of serving as a faculty member, a kind of obedience for the sake of the common good. In both Catholic and university divinity school situations, there are typically term limits which distinguish these calls from those that "serve at the pleasure of the board."

There is also a *visionary call*. When approached by a search committee, or even when requested to submit one's name for consideration, some are caught up with the excitement of being able to create something new. While all candidates for the office no doubt cherish dreams and hopes for the enterprise, some are more highly motivated by these dreams than others. They may assume that current ways of doing theological education are obsolete; they believe their vision can make significant changes and thus contribute uniquely to the shape of the ministry of the church in the next century. Such visions should be tempered by a realistic view of the intransigence of educational communities when it comes to changing their own ways. It is nonetheless true, however, that persons without dreams and hopes are not inspiring leaders.

We might refer to the visionary calling as the *ministry call* since most of the dreams relate to a hope of strengthening church ministry. There might be a slight difference, however, in that some are not necessarily motivated by a need to change everything; they simply see the task of preparing persons for the ministry of the church as exciting. One president spoke passionately of preparing leadership for the church as the single most important thing a person who loves the church could do. This, he affirmed, was the call that came to him through the presidential search committee.

There are persons who experience a *"can do" calling*. These persons know they have certain gifts that have been honed in other settings and could be used in the presidency of a seminary. They may be "insiders" or "outsiders" who happen to know something about theological education because of their positions and/or previous experience. They feel at home with what they are going to be called upon to do; they enjoy the type of work the position entails. They sense a "fit" with the office.

The internal calling, the sense of God's will in the invitation to the office, therefore, can come through a community, a vision, a commitment to obedience, hopes for ministry, and a sense of the fact that God has prepared one for the job. These may not be separate callings, but facets of the one call a person receives while interacting with the institution.

THE GIFTS

We have seen that there is no such thing as *the* presidency and it should be obvious there is no such thing as particular gifts or talents or experience that will infallibly guarantee a person will be a good president. But it is equally clear that a person's faith, gifts, experience, and temperament do matter even though there may not be one configuration of features that is "foolproof."

There are some rather obvious things a person and a search committee can ask when trying to decide about the fit between a candidate and a position. How committed is the candidate to the task of theological education? How much does the person know about the life and history of the institution? Is the person skillful in working with people and does she enjoy doing so? Has the person had any administrative experience? Certainly trustees should have in mind the particular needs of the institution at this juncture in its life and bring to the attention of candidates aspects of the work which are likely to be prominent. Is the person gifted with incredible amounts of energy, stamina, and vitality? Still, having said this, we are still left with no simple answers.

David Nygren, in a study of leaders of Catholic religious institutions, notes there are such things as "threshold competencies," meaning the gifts needed to sustain an institution. For example, the person should be mission oriented, enjoy seeing goals fulfilled, able to administer the operation, willing to seek information that enables him or her to function more effectively, and the like. But then he speaks of the traits of outstanding leaders, persons judged by their peers as above average in institutional leadership. This list includes being very achievement oriented and engaging actively in planning ahead, taking the initiative in solving problems, not waiting until they fester. The person is able to mobilize others to attain the group's goals; is sensitive to the needs of others, but is primarily focused on the institution's goals. An outstanding leader shows signs of greater spiritual sensitivity, sees the spiritual significance of events, and is aware of the presence of God in individual lives and the events of the school.[3]

Many of Nygren's traits are congruent with our understanding of educational leadership, but his work is particularly interesting because of the latter trait he mentions. It seems to agree with what others have observed on a less scientific level; that is, persons who make good seminary presidents are persons of faith, persons who are deeply committed, for whom God is a real factor. This is certainly not to downplay the other factors, but to call attention to the prominence of this particular one.

In addition to Nygren's list of competencies, I have tried to identify some of the demands the office places on a president's personality. How does the person typically respond to pressure, or criticism? Is the person able to combine thinking and action in order to learn? Using somewhat unorthodox and clearly unscientific categories, my list is intended to provoke reflection about a *person*, one considering the presidency, or one presently in office.[4] These categories may assist search committees in evaluating a candidate's style of interaction with the seminary community.

Engagement and Reflection. What stimulates a person's mind and heart? For some it is mixing doing with reading, or action with reflection. These people actually may think better while engaged in doing. While everyone needs time alone to reflect and think (see the following), presidents need to be able to enjoy the activities they are called upon to do and use them to prompt reflection on the institution's mission and purpose. This is an approach to living, vocation, and mission. It might, indeed, be another way of talking about the president as the one who teaches and designs learning experiences in the midst of the give and take of the office.

People and Solitude. A president has to be gregarious. The job demands teamwork; the life is one of constant engagement with other human beings. But because there is an essentially lonely aspect to the job, a president had better be able to be alone for the inner nurture that comes with meditation, prayer, and reflection. It is not only for one's inner strength that solitude is necessary, but also for the good of the institution. It is difficult to reflect before God about the future of the school and its mission in today's world, when there is a cacophony of voices vying for one's attention. These voices are necessary, but so is the solitude that brings the possibility of mature judgment to the weighty issues confronting such a leader.

Justice and Confidentiality. Every person has preferences and biases. We like some people; others turn us off. We think one academic subject or department is more important to the life of the school than others; one cannot help having these convictions. But the most certain path to a ruined presidency is to show favoritism in the administration of an institution. To operate with an even hand, to be just, is exceedingly difficult, but absolutely necessary.

It is in the efforts to administer justice that we are likewise called upon to practice confidentiality. A president frequently knows more about the personal lives of faculty and staff than anyone in the institution; he does, after all, function as a pastor. Because of his position, he probably reads the evaluations of more people than anyone else. When a person's contract is not renewed or someone is asked to leave, the president on occasion must take abuse from members of the community because of the necessity to retain confidentiality. There are times when reasons cannot be shared publicly. Administering justice and maintaining confidentiality go hand in hand.

Stability and Change. The political, social, and ecclesiastical worlds around the theological school shift and change. Schools are constantly having to make adjustments, either because they are financially strapped or are expanding. For the stability of the institution, lines of authority and responsibility must be clear, job descriptions up to date, policies in good order. Keeping these things current is an unending task, but one that must be pursued with diligence. Management, as we have seen, is very important. Yet changes in the world call upon institutions to be open to the new, to adjust, to make alterations, both small and large. Bringing about such change is what we have labeled as leadership. To work for this while maintaining a sense of stability within the institution is a difficult and crucial balance.

Convictions and Openness. One needs a vision of what theological education is all about. What are the important issues for the life of this school and what is ephemeral? Presidents need strong convictions about God, the church, the ministry, and God's world. Yet presidents are in office to help schools fulfill their vocations, live out their histories, serve trustees, faculty, graduates, and the church. So presidents also need to be open to the convictions of others; otherwise they will not grow, nor will they serve the people whom God has called them to serve. Remaining faithful to one's commitments while being open to the convictions of others is not easy since convictions tend to define one's reality. There can be no building of mutual purposes—the goal of leadership—without this sharing of self and openness to others.

Selfish and Selfless. When talking about leadership in the church, the word servant is often used. This is one who does not ask to be served, but is there to serve—not as a doormat, letting people trample on him, but rather going places he does not necessarily want to go with people he does not particularly want to be with. Much presidential work is activity the person would not choose. But presidents must draw lines; they must take care of themselves. Since there is frequently no one else to do this, presidents must learn to take the type of breaks *they* need, find time to read and reflect, schedule family events. Selfish is probably not the best word, but the point is clear. Presidents do give of themselves for the sake of the institution and the cause of Christ, but they also must know how to love themselves, or the whirling chaos of demands will consume them.

Focus and Diffusion. There are so many kinds of things that must be done—selling property, dealing with church executives, wrestling with government regulations, enduring pettiness. At the same time one must maintain a focus. One needs to be able to isolate the unique things that only a president can do, focus on these, and let others carry the primary responsibilities for the rest. Maintaining the vision, nurturing the best in the institution's ethos, shepherding the board, remembering the future possibilities of the institution—these are the types of things that should be the focal point for presidents. Delegating to executive staff and managers while identifying those crucial changes that one wants to undertake is a sign of leadership.

These are typical demands made upon presidents. There is nothing sacred about the list; others could be added. The ones that have been selected point to types of interactions presidents have with their environments. They may not require specific gifts, but they point to characteristics of persons who are able to enjoy the work of the presidency and function effectively as educators.

THE SUPPORT

Presidents do not say much about this matter. Nevertheless, I believe it is one of the few things that can make the difference between a helpful, successful presidency and a failure. While the support and care of presidents must be tailored to the person, I will suggest a typical board structure that can help, along with some more informal approaches that can be taken.

Board Structure. As a way of providing support for the president, trustees in one institution formed a Personnel Committee. Their belief was that personnel matters within the school were to be attended to by the administration. Their Personnel Committee was to deal with the president alone. They would do informal reviews of the president's service every year and oversee a more substantial review every third year. This group set the president's salary. In doing this, they ordinarily reviewed the salaries of the senior staff members who reported to the president; thus they could keep the institution's salary scale in balance.

They also developed a "Presidential Leave Policy." They were careful not to call it a sabbatic leave, which implies a certain schedule of work and writing. The policy allowed for a month's leave, in addition to the vacation period, for every year of service. These leave months could be accumulated, but the president was never to be away during one academic year for more than six months, including vacation. Thus the president had considerable flexibility. Two months every year—one for vacation and one for presidential leave; or, the vacation only for one or two years, and then a leave of three or four months.

While the president was expected to discuss the leave plans with this group, he did not have to write reports or carry out particular projects. If he happened to be in serious need of rest, he could simply do that. Or, he could travel, using such trips to augment the school's reputation and recruiting efforts. He might want to spend the time catching up on reading, either in his academic discipline or in areas directly related to his work as president. He might even want to complete some writing he had been working on for years.

There are people who say they cannot relax and forget the office unless they are away at least a month. Others like shorter periods, even a long weekend can provide the break they find satisfying; people have different rhythms for "changing gears" or relaxing. The policy established by this committee gave room for flexibility.

The president's well being is at stake, and this means the institution's health is at stake. The committee and the president need to discuss anything and everything that either the president or the committee believes is important. Certainly, from the first meeting on, they should discuss the president's leaving office. This may sound strange, but I believe it sets the context for a healthy relationship and frees the president to consider future options and even create some of the same. More will be said about this later.

In our example, the Personnel Committee, which consisted of only four or five persons, would convene to hear the president share a perplexing situation he was facing, one that might have broad political ramifications among constituencies. They were a sounding board for subjects he did not want to discuss in a formal setting. Under such circumstances, one or more of these folk might well become a close personal friend of the president with whom he could feel free to share anything. There are those who believe that the chair of the board is the one with whom the president should develop a uniquely personal relation. At times, the chair of the board does not live near enough to allow for this relationship; in this situation or in certain other circumstances, some other trustee should fulfill this role.

While the Personnel Committee structure is only one way of approaching support of the president, some such arrangement needs to be in place. This may change with each occupant of the office since no two people need the same kind of support. However, unless there is a group whose specific assignment is to watch after the president, such care will likely be neglected. The salary, the perks, the role of the spouse, the need for rest, the questions about the family—these are all matters that deserve careful attention.

Informal Structures. Presidents who come to the office after serving on the faculty find that the old relations and friendships are no longer there. The camaraderie of the department and the admiration of students are gone. People who come from pastorates also find the circle of friends and recognition they received in their communities have vanished for all practical purposes. People tell pastors on Sundays that the sermon was helpful, they thank them for sharing in a funeral of a loved one, or they celebrate with them at their daughter's wedding. By contrast, one president reports that even though his spouse worked very hard to entertain the faculty and their spouses at dinner, she was seldom thanked at the end of the evening. There was an attitude that suggested the president and spouse *owed* this to the community. Another president told of going to an elaborate function at the local museum shortly after he had assumed office. No one in the group knew who he was; both he and his wife were unknown. When he told people who he was, they were not familiar with the seminary. He had been a well known figure as pastor of a distinguished church in another city and this anonymity was uncomfortable. He realized he would probably never be as well known in the new community, even if he stayed for fifteen years. The seminary would never be as prominent as his local church had been.

Ways must be found to help presidents sense the support and care of others. Presidents of secular institutions appear to find a great source of comfort and support in being able to talk with others in similar positions. Seminary presidents seem far more hesitant to do this. Is it because they are perfectionists and feel such confession of pain or confusion would be indications of failure? Is it because they sense a kind of competition with other seminary presidents? The answers to these questions are unknown. Distance, the press of time, and other factors may play a role; and certainly there are exceptions to this general observation.

Some presidents are able to share openly with key staff members; they do so with complete confidence that their conversations, rehearsing of scenarios, evaluations of persons, will never be mentioned to anyone else. Presidents tell of having one, two, or three trustees whom they trust implicitly; they frequently share with these persons and find the conversations not only clarifying but also psychologically satisfying. When someone a president esteems highly says that a recent decision appears to have been taken too hastily or without adequate preparation, she tends to listen. If these same friends tell the president her weariness is showing and suggest she consider a short break, she is likely to take their advice.

The emphasis in this section is clearly upon the trustees, though I do not want to limit the president's support to them. But trustees are the special people who are ordinarily in a unique position to offer the president support and care. Not all of this is organized or planned. For example, from time to time one trustee sent a beautiful blooming azalea or an orchid plant to the president and his spouse. A special letter, a public commendation, a gracious offer to do some task ordinarily left to the president, a word of appreciation at faculty meetings—all of these gestures and kindnesses can gently support those who need that encouragement.

Over the years seminary presidents have not been immunized against the alcoholism, divorce, and mental breakdowns that plague persons in every profession who live with stress and pressure. Having built-in systems for support may go far in helping the president avoid some of these common, destructive consequences of the position.

THE REVIEW

Should presidents be evaluated? It would seem natural in light of the fact that in academic communities, faculty members are reviewed for promotion and tenure according to schedule; students are reviewed or evaluated at stated times, as are members of the staff in most situations. If the president is to be thought of as an educator, why should he not be evaluated like everyone else? A few years ago when Leon Pacala did a study of seminary presidents, he found that 80 percent did have reviews, and that 70 percent of these were done by the governing board.[5]

But why evaluate a president? She is not up for promotion and there is no lifelong tenure associated with the position. If one thinks of only *summative* evaluation, which tells what and how one did in the past, the process has obvious limits. But if we are to think in terms of *formative* evaluation, that is, evaluation that occurs during the process so that improvement and change might take place while the activity is happening, then the review is far more constructive.[6] The review process sheds light on the president, yes, but it also may reveal something about the governing board and clarify the goals of the institution.

Purpose. John W. Nason suggests the following purposes for presidential reviews: (1) to fulfill the board's responsibility; (2) to strengthen the president's position and improve performance; (3) to review and improve the governance of the institution; (4) to review and reset institutional goals; (5) to educate trustees, faculty, and others on the president's role; (6) to decide whether to retain or fire; (7) to set an example for faculty and staff evaluations; (8) to set salary.[7] Of all of these, I suspect that number five may be the most important.

Structure. Persons who have studied the matter of presidential evaluations favor an informal review rather than a formal one which usually includes asking persons to take part who do not have the slightest idea about what a president does. Formal reviews tend to provide everyone in the community who has a grievance an opportunity to air it.

The proposal to have an informal trustee review, say by the Personnel Committee, on an annual basis appears to be the preferred approach. Perhaps a more formal review could be done every three to five years.[8] If the latter is done, consideration should be given to distributing questionnaires that contain categories of presidential responsibility. If these are selected with care they can actually teach the persons who use them something about the president's job.

If the board is basically pleased with the president's performance, the materials sent out as part of the review can contain statements like these: "The Board of Trustees believes President Jones is doing a fine job. Like all of us, however, she would like feedback as to how others perceive her performance. We are assisting her with this task as well as gathering data for our own evaluation. We have listed some of the areas of responsibility and would appreciate your frank response. If you are unfamiliar with the president's work in any of these areas, please indicate."

In addition it is possible to develop different instruments for different constituencies. Students ordinarily have no idea how the president relates to donors; maintenance staff are not likely to attend meetings of board committees; faculty members may not know how the president relates to senior staff. Such tailored questionnaires prevent persons from speaking to areas in which they have no firsthand knowledge and yet involves the larger community in the evaluation.

At the conclusion of the review, assuming the board is basically satisfied with the president's performance, a letter should be sent to all of those participating and perhaps to the entire community. It should contain the affirmation of the board and, on occasion, a list of particulars the board is asking the president to focus on during the coming years. This again supports the president and also informs the community of the president's tasks.

The dangers as well as the possibilities of such reviews are discussed in detail by Nason in his book, *Presidential Assessment.*[9]

THE PRICE

There is a price one pays for every significant decision. If one decides to marry this person, others are excluded. If one enters academia, the option of becoming wealthy is probably rejected. If one purchases a large car, one pays for the gas. Such is life. What price does one pay when deciding to become a president?

Loneliness. At several places in this book we have mentioned the loneliness of the president's office. Not everyone feels this as much as others, but the nature of the position tends to cut one off from certain groups and clearly puts the pressure of one's decisions in one's own lap.

Academic Discipline. Many presidents have Ph.D.s and have taught in a given field. The rapidity with which knowledge increases in our time is a popular topic and a true one. Presidents find it difficult to read scholarly journals in their chosen field, to keep abreast of major publications in the discipline, and to attend meetings of fellow scholars to hear papers on recent research. Thus, a president is likely to sense his competence in his field gradually eroding. If the field happens to be some branch of ethics or education or management, he might be able to use much of what he has learned over the years and even see relationships with what he is doing. But to assume he could teach or write with the expertise he had before taking on the current job of president is usually not true.

Some presidents are able to arrange their schedules and lives so they can maintain their scholarly pursuits. One such person studied every night from 8p.m. until 1:30a.m. Most presidents cannot be home by eight every evening because of the demands for entertainment, meetings, and travel. They must find satisfaction in realizing that they are continuing to be teachers and educators, but in the sense in which we have discussed earlier.

Family. Persons in high profile and demanding jobs frequently have family problems. This is true even in our time when one's spouse is not necessarily assumed to be the unpaid "assistant" to the president. A seminary president once spoke of the large amount of entertaining he and his wife did. He noted it was a "mom and pop" operation. They bought the food, cooked it, served it, and cleaned up afterwards. This can be a tiring task!

Roberta Ostar argues that the public role of the president's family is often not appreciated. They become "living logos" of the institution and "market" the school by becoming involved in a wide variety of community activities. The spouse will attend one meeting so the school is represented while the president is at another meeting. The friendships built, the trust developed, the contacts made are a significant part of nurturing constituencies which are so vital to a school's life. In addition, staff and others may want to come to the president's home for a Christmas party as being there means something special to them. While many presidential families do not feel the president's house is *their* home, one should beware of spending money on it so that better entertaining can take place; this is likely to cause a storm![10] In short, the family is pulled into the orbit of the job regardless of efforts to see that this does not happen, or at least not in a destructive fashion.

In today's world, the spouse of the president is likely to have a career of his or her own. The president must learn to adjust the entertaining duties, perhaps using caterers or private clubs, though many institutions lack funds for this. Without a career outside the home, the spouse's personal life is clearly affected. The president needs psychological support; household responsibilities and social functions frequently clash. Knowing when and how much of the president's job to share is not always easy. However the arrangements are made to handle these various dilemmas, there will be a price to pay as well as many good times with fascinating friends. But when one's spouse cannot sleep because of worries or is away traveling for the seminary, there is indeed a price to be paid by the entire family.[11]

These family matters clearly need to be discussed *before* a person accepts a call and then on a continuing basis.

Physical and Psychological Pressure. A great many presidents experienced "burnout" before the phrase came into being.[12] Now it is commonly used to describe the physical wear and tear of the job as well as psychological stress. The presidency is not the only job with these kind of pressures, but ordinarily seminary staffs are thin and much of the work that would be handed on to others must be carried by the president.

The smallness of theological schools, the close living quarters in many cases, and the deep convictions about doctrine and social attitudes held by faculty and students combine to make life in these institutions uncommonly tense. The same decision made in the context of a major university without a ripple can cause an emotional uproar in these small settings. At a university some vice president for personnel or dean of a college may be a target for lightning, while the president is often spared. But in seminaries, the president is more often than not the person blamed for whatever happens.

The stress is not always caused by personal disagreements. The mere fact of having to cut a budget by fifteen percent brings with it stress and pain; the inability to get the supporting church to make needed changes generates frustration. Clearly the job brings with it a certain amount of wear and tear. More will be said about some of these problems and why the job is so difficult in Chapter 7.

THE JOYS

Two former presidents, writing independently of each other, spoke of their optimism. One said he thought presidents tended to be the kind of people who lived by hope, who were basically optimistic about life, whether due to their faith or just their human makeup. The other warned that we have to be careful not to confuse innate chemical optimism with biblical hope! Apparently many presidents have both, for presidents as a group are happy people. They enjoy their work.

A president described the types of varied activities in which he engaged in any one day, and then noted how much he liked this kind of life. He thrived on variety, many types of responsibilities and activities. Having one's schedule interrupted, talking with all manner of folk on the telephone, corresponding with bishops as well as an unknown donor living on an island in Alaska, leading worship and eating with students in the refectory. There are people who enjoy this kind of life.

Harvey Guthrie, President and Dean of Episcopal Divinity School for many years, spoke of the profound satisfaction of living out the school's unique and interesting history within the Episcopal Church. As an Old Testament scholar, Guthrie was sensitive to the way culture influences institutions and thus could see his own ministry as being similar to that of the prophets. Knowing the history, living and reliving the history of an institution is meaningful.

One of the joys of the presidency is "growing an institution." The president is perhaps the only person aware of the various dimensions of a school's life. She shares the excitement of seeing visions become reality, hopes being fulfilled, and dreams materializing. She shares in the maturing of the board; adding good faculty members; gathering a new group of promising students each year; securing better financial support; increasing academic resources such as the library and media. She sees it all as it fits together into a whole that is focused on a purpose.

There is also the downside of this; the president has to help the institution redefine its purpose, change course, and become smaller but more focused in its work. Retrenchment is seldom popular. If it is seen as the elimination of programs and persons unpopular with the president, then the institution's integrity is questioned. But if downsizing can be done with dialogue and compassion, then even this task can bring satisfaction, for it will be helping the institution be what it can be in this day.

The expressions of joy are numerous. In some cases the president becomes the leader of a worshiping community; in others he models ministry for a generation of students. As one president said: Where else can you have so much influence over so many people? Not just your trustees, faculty, and students but, through them, people in churches all over the world.

In a highly practical vein, President Barbara Brown Zikmund of Hartford Seminary has indicated that she found great satisfaction in "keeping all the balls in the air...dealing with complex difficult issues in a humane way...being an effective ambassador for the Seminary...helping new friends understand our program...turning around a disgruntled alumnus/ a...learning about the history of the various institutions that are part of our history and the creative way in which the story of the Seminary has unfolded...modeling the fact that a woman can exercise institutional leadership in a collaborative and transformational way...strengthening clergy in their ministries so that they can enliven tired congregations and revitalize themselves as Christian leaders." [13] Who could ask for more?

I hope trustees, either in committee or as individuals, will consider the joys of the presidency and seek to enhance these dimensions of the job.

THE EXIT

As I have observed frequently, every presidency is different. This is true when it comes to deciding when to leave the office. For some it is no problem; they are on a term appointment which cannot be renewed. Others who lose the support of the board and/or faculty are asked to leave. Some reach retirement age and depart accordingly. There are still others who receive a call to a new work; for them, the question is the appropriateness of leaving at a certain time. Whatever the circumstances, presidents have to ask themselves from time to time about their plans to depart.

There is no simple answer to the question of departure, but the reading of many memoirs and discussions with numerous presidents provide some hints. For example, a president may notice that a cycle in the life of the school is drawing to an end. The new buildings are completed; the endowment has been tripled; the faculty is about to experience a large number of retirements and the task of calling a practically new faculty is facing someone. Cycles in the life of a school are not always so clear, but a president who is alert to the ebb and flow of life within the community can frequently identify a time when the departure of one president and the coming of another would be advantageous for the school.

Another clear signal is the loss of support of the board and/or faculty. One president says that with every major decision he had to make, he lost considerable support within one of these groups. This is true of everyone to some extent. A president who does not have the trust and confidence of the members of the community cannot lead.

Many years ago, Duke McCall, then president of Southern Baptist Seminary in Louisville said: "Fatigue is the great enemy of the president." When one is bone weary, one does not make good decisions or attack problems with energy and enthusiasm. A president tells of returning from a sabbatic only to realize how weary he was of dealing with the same personnel and financial problems that had confronted him for years. He experienced a strong sense of not wanting to go on.

A friend taught me an interesting truth about growing weary of dealing with the routine, with the same problems year in and year out. "One is likely to begin to withdraw a bit from first this area of the school's life and then that one," he said. "Just let the faculty do as they please about this or that; had I the energy, I would reason with them to see if we could not change this just a little. Or, there is no need to spend so much time preparing for the board meeting; we get along so well. Or, my staff is so good I don't think I'll give them an annual review this year." The urge to educate was waning.

As a president withdraws that constant watchfulness, that gentle persuasion, that persistent reclaiming of the purpose, that careful listening to colleagues, that critique of the use of funds—a vacuum forms that pulls others in to replace the president's influence. This usurpation of presidential prerogatives and role is done unconsciously for the most part. A tired president is glad to see someone else "taking a lead." But the school begins to suffer from lack of leadership and mild forms of chaos begin to breed. Some trustee is now meddling a bit too much in the administration of the school; a faculty member is pressing for a policy she has tried to get passed for years. Some students are visiting with staff and making suggestions about work conditions. No one may be doing anything wrong necessarily; folk are simply filling the vacuum created by a tired president's gradual withdrawal from the life of the school.

One hopes the president will have those regular conferences with the good friend or friends we mentioned earlier. He or she may not see the withdrawal, may not even be conscious of the void being created. Others are more likely to perceive it and let the president know it is time to leave. Remaining in office while actually withdrawing generates confusion and erosion of gains so dearly made over a period of years. I believe this is why new presidents frequently comment: "I heard this place had been well run by my predecessor, but things are in a mess!" Both parts of the statement are probably true. It had been managed carefully over the years, but a vacuum, caused either by a tired president or a gap between presidents, allowed conditions to deteriorate.

We noted earlier that some presidents reach retirement age and step aside. This means the age at which one assumes the office is important to the individual as well as to the board. If one becomes president while in one's forties, the expectation might well be to find another position upon leaving the presidency. If one enters the office in the mid-fifties, one might expect to stay until retirement. These age differences should be discussed from the beginning of a candidate's courtship with an institution.

What happens when a president completes his tenure before the age of retirement? With many Catholics, the decision about future employment is negotiated with the person's bishop or superior. In university divinity schools, the dean frequently has tenure as a professor and can remain on the faculty as a regular professor. This of course can happen in freestanding schools, but does not appear to be as standard a procedure as in the case of the universities.

A few presidents move from CEO of one theological institution to another. This does not happen often, either because age or the fact that presidents are too weary to take on a new position like the one they are leaving. Some presidents move into administration in either ecclesiastical bureaucracies or educational associations, such as accrediting agencies, or the National Catholic Educational Association, or perhaps as an executive in the office for theological education of a denomination. They can thus use their experience as president in a new setting. Some leave academia all together; they return to the pastorate or an entirely different line of work, such as a foundation executive.

Under the section on support of the president I mentioned the importance of talking about departure from the very day one arrives. I have heard people say they never discuss leaving because they are so delighted with their current work; they find every day a challenge. I will not doubt what they say, but I do not believe this is a good reason to avoid the subject, at least on an annual basis. Such conversations can greatly increase the possibilities of leaving in an orderly fashion and with some clear career move in mind.

CONCLUSION

The importance of the person occupying the office cannot be overstated. Those who enter the presidency, sensing a call of God, undertake a vocation that defies outcomes based on the person's competencies, traits, and experience. These are not unimportant, but there is no one combination of gifts and training that will guarantee a successful presidency. The more a search committee knows about a candidate, the more the candidate knows about the institution, the better are the prospects for a good and useful match of person with position.

But each human being has distinctive capacities for being with others and being alone, for acting and thinking, for firmness and flexibility, for enduring hurt and experiencing hope. It is out of this singular mixture of gifts and education that a person exercises presidential leadership. Knowing the stress that goes with institutional leadership in this age, trustees will act wisely if they build in support tailored to the uniqueness of the individual. This might well include a helpful review which offers feedback as well as public affirmation. Regardless of the compatibility of the person and the office, however, and assuming good support, the position still will cost the president at some point. But the joys of the calling are equally real and satisfying. Even a person's departure from the office can be an occasion for celebration and renewal in the life of the school and the retiring president.

NOTES

[1] Clark Kerr and Marian Gade,*The Many Lives of Presidents*, 172

[2] Mark Allyn Holman, *Presidential Search in Theological Schools: Process Makes a Difference.* 1994. Published privately and available through the ATS.

[3] David J. Nygren,C.M., *et al*, "Religious-Leadership Competencies" in *Review for Religious* (May-June,1993) 390-417.

[4] I put this list together after reading a provocative article by the former president of Union Theological Seminary in New York, Donald W. Shriver, Jr., "Visions and Nightmares: The Leader's Call to See Reality—and Change It". *In Trust* (New Year, 1992), 16-20. Some of the material is clearly taken from the article.

[5] Leon Pacala, op. cit., 17-18, 39-41.

[6] C. Ellis Nelson, *Using Evaluation in Theological Education* (Nashville: Discipleship Resources), 1975.

[7] John W. Nason, assisted by Nancy Axelrod, *Presidential Assessment* (Washington, D. C.: Association of Governing Boards, 1984), 9-12.

[8] James Fisher suggests using an outside consultant for this major review. See his *The Board and the President* (New York: MacMillan, American Council on Education, 1991), Chapter 7, especially 77-79.

[9] Clark Kerr has a chapter on this subject also in his *Presidents Make a Difference*, Chapter 5. See also James L. Fisher, *The Board and the President*, Chapter 7.

[10] Roberta Ostar, *Public Roles, Private Lives: The Representational Role of College and University Presidents* (Washington, D. C.: Association of Governing Boards, 1991), Special Report.

[11] Kerr and Gade, *The Many Lives of Academic Presidents*, 116-117.

[12] Peter Drucker says something very interesting about "burnout" in his book *Managing the Non-Profit Organization* (New York: HarperCollins, 1990): " `Burnout,' much of the time, is a cop out for being bored. Nothing creates more fatigue than having to force yourself to go to work in the morning when you don't give a damn." 197.

[13] Barbara Brown Zikmund's paper for this project. Her list of satisfactions is much longer than the quotation here; this abbreviated form is quoted with permission.

7

SYSTEMIC PROBLEMS

A successful president who retired after fourteen years observed: "It's a tough job...no man in his right mind...would purposely prepare himself to be the dean or the president of a seminary." A seminary trustee, the chief administrative officer for one of American's major corporations, remarked that the seminary president's job was much more complicated and difficult than his.

Previous chapters have pointed to some of the difficulties the CEO of a theological institution encounters. In this chapter I want to draw attention to *systemic* problems, difficulties that are inherent in the structures of the institutions and those that support the seminaries. Even though I have suggested certain perspectives and redefinitions of the president's tasks, it should nonetheless be noted that "it's a tough job."

Pointing to systemic problems is another way of remembering that not all of the problems seminaries experience are rooted in the personality and gifts of the president. Some presidents, being perfectionists, seem to believe this; they blame themselves for everything that happens in the institution. There is a tendency for others in the community to do the same, yet our analysis will indicate that some problems are systemic; that is, they exist regardless of who is president, for they are built into the structures of the school or the supporting institutions.

HYBRID INSTITUTIONS

Theological schools belong both to the church and to the academy.[1] They are institutions dedicated to serving the Christian faith and to intellectually pursuing the truth. Over the centuries the marriage of

Jerusalem and Athens has been a rocky one. In the best of all worlds the two should live together in harmony, but that has not always been the case. Seminaries were created in North America to prepare persons for service in the churches and communities. This preparation involved the formation of the person, the acquiring of the "mind of Christ," the transformation of the self by renewing the mind. Academic study, reflection on documents, and wrestling with truth were parts of the process. Seminaries have been called "schools of the prophets," and *schools* engage in serious cognitive activities. The academic preparation of the faculty, the size of the library, and the shape of the curriculum were the essence of an institution. Faculty members were expected to produce scholarly literature for the sake of the faith. The first seminary, Andover, contained the beginnings of professional academic groups, especially in the area of biblical studies; the faculty deliberately prepared others for the task of teaching. The same was true of some of the other early seminaries. The ecclesial and academic commitments meshed together in those early days without apparent conflict.

In our own time, the ecclesial commitment of schools is expressed in the content of the theology that is taught, the common life of worship and piety, which reflects the tradition, and the commitments of the faculty. David Kelsey writes about the powerful impact the view of the Christian faith believed by a particular seminary community has on its whole life.[2] He also demonstrates how a particular educational model adopted consciously or unconsciously by the school affects its life. Faith commitments and the educational process are not two different things, but blend together in the life of an institution. The tensions, conflicts, possibilities, and problems of this marriage have been helpfully traced by Edward Farley, David Kelsey and others.[3] Our purpose is not to rehearse this history but to glimpse the problems created for presidents by the hybrid nature of the institutions they serve. We are thus looking at symptoms of the problem, not the underlying issues.

For example, the president has to deal with the *political* ramifications of the hybrid institution. On the one hand the president may be badgered by church judicatory leaders with a barrage of statements like these: your graduates know many details of biblical criticism, but do not understand the dynamics of teaching the Bible to a group of laypersons; your students have no idea how to lead worship or preach a good sermon; they are ignorant of our church polity; they understand nothing about church budgets.

On the other hand, the president hears from the faculty: the professor of Old Testament blames the students' lack of knowledge on the crowded curriculum which allows her only one required course; the professor of social ethics, noting that he has no required courses, is deeply buried in his own research on genetic engineering; the theology professor is requesting a term off so she can complete her book; the faculty in the "practical department" (preaching, teaching and counseling) lament not having time for practicums needed to prepare persons for their chosen vocation. Students meanwhile agitate for more opportunities for sharing the Eucharist and complain that few of the faculty attend chapel.

While questions like the relation of theory to practice underlie much of the ongoing discussion about the nature of theological education, the president is located at the crossroads where grievances are aired, grievances which frequently reflect such underlying issues. The church wants graduates to be prepared to lead congregations; the faculty wants respectable academic requirements and scholarly professors. The complaints are serious ones, whether voiced by the church or the faculty. Both have legitimate claims on the seminary; both are involved in the politics of the school, but the president alone cannot solve the dilemmas. Pressures from churches can involve withholding funds as well as sending students to other institutions. Accrediting societies can withhold accreditation if academic standards are neglected and good faculty can move to other institutions. The president does not create these pressures, but *it is the president* who must live with them.

A second area in which tensions between church commitments and academic orientation emerge might be called *vocational*. Students preparing for a life of service in some form of ministry study the Scriptures, for example, as a resource for personal faith and the life of the community. They hope their study of theology will not only enable them to know what previous generations of believers have confessed, but also equip them to state their own faith with clarity in light of the issues of our time. They expect their study of prayer will enable them to pray personally and lead the people of God in prayer. Youth ministry and pastoral counseling are seen as means for carrying ministry to persons with specific needs. This is, after all, why they came to seminary in the first place.

Faculty members, by contrast, have spent years gaining the Ph.D. so they could be accredited to teach. They were selected because of their field of specialization and promoted based on scholarly work. They *may* prefer to study Scripture with a major focus on rhetorical criticism, or see youth ministry as a sophisticated investigation of developmental stages, or view prayer in the context of the history of spirituality. But schools want faculty members to participate in programs for laity, fund raisers, alumni/ae meetings, chapel services, open houses, and softball teams. They might be asked to share their personal faith journeys with students in the evening in their homes. The academic matters—good scholarship, areas of research, writing book reviews—are expressions of their guilds, their professional lives which frequently seem far removed from their work. Yet the theological school, as servant of the church, is making demands on these people which divert them from their academic commitments and careers.

These various perspectives stated may be caricatures, but there is no question about the conflict engendered by the hybrid nature of the seminary with respect to vocations. Once again, the president is the focal point for the legitimate concerns of students, church supporters, and faculty.

There is also a *philosophical* problem that expresses itself in concrete ways. A church institution frequently requires the president and faculty to subscribe to the confessional position of the supporting church. This may take the form of an installation service in which the person is asked to affirm the confession of the tradition as his or her own faith. Or, it may mean that only persons ordained in the particular tradition are invited to join the faculty; the ordaining body thus guarantees their orthodoxy. In other schools, there are creedal statements written by the founders or trustees which all faculty must agree to and be willing to report any deviation from the creed that may occur in their thinking. The problem arises when this commitment to a version of the truth is confronted with the matter of academic freedom, the belief that faculty members should be free to pursue the truth wherever it leads. Many assume professors should be guaranteed the right to publish their findings without fear of recrimination, including loss of job.

Again it is the president who stands between the church, with its justifiable concerns, and the faculty who rightly want to seek the truth without fear or intimidation. There are ways to deal with these tensions,[4] but the pressure that arises from this dual commitment of the institution presents the president with trying situations.

The presence of these tensions, however, can be healthy as well as trying. They encourage people to lift afresh the question of the institution's basic purpose; they help some institutions avoid the provincialism that comes from isolation in their own traditions; they remind even the most academically-oriented seminary of the claims of God's people on their lives and the life of the institution.

One additional word. In today's church and academy there are a host of special interest groups. Depending on the ecclesial relations and the context of the school, there can be groups who want changes in faculty, curriculum, financial aid programs, and housing arrangements, to name a few. These groups may represent conservatives or liberals, gays, lesbians or straights, males or females, minorities or Caucasians; many of them can bring incredible pressure to bear to accomplish their objectives. Being a hybrid institution tends to compound the numbers of these groups, not lessen them.

Inherent in the hybrid nature of the theological institution are built-in difficulties for the president.

ORIENTATION

I am applying the word *orientation* in two ways. First, I am using it to refer to a person's grasp of a job, based on either experiences, or knowledge gained from an educational program designed to prepare persons for a specific type of work. Second, I am using the word to refer to a person's own disposition toward the job to be done.

In our discussion of the personal orientation of the people who become seminary presidents, we have noted that they come primarily from the academic world or the pastorate. Yet academia is well known for developing persons who work in highly individualistic ways, who are commonly unaware of the nature of institutions (though there obviously are exceptions to this, depending on one's discipline), and who have found that teaching, research, and writing bring them their greatest rewards. We have noted earlier that among academics administration is commonly viewed with disdain. We have also noted that this same attitude frequently exists among clergy, though many of them have had administrative duties whether they liked them or not. Despite this prevalent personal disposition, persons who accept the presidency of an institution apparently have some feel for administration and must have been involved sufficiently to believe they can do it and even like it. The exception to this may be the rector or faculty member who accepts the job out of obedience, either to a superior or colleagues. The presidency of seminaries is one of the few vocations that calls people whose personal orientation is frequently foreign to that of the position.

But having accepted the job, presidents begin to cast about for some orientation program, some way to learn about their responsibilities. Most presidents who wrote memoirs for this project indicated they had to learn from scratch while doing the work. Neither their predecessor nor an adequate job description was available. One dean of a university divinity school recalled that a long-time secretary in the office guided him, since he had no idea what he was supposed to do either within the divinity school or the university. A rector told of having been on the faculty for twelve years before assuming office; yet he says he had very little idea of what the rector's job was like until he walked into the office.

Another rector, who had been on the faculty of the school which he now heads, noted it was not until he read several books that analyzed the nature of organizations and how they work that he had the foggiest notion of his task. Though familiar with the school, he was not aware of the subtleties of nurturing and managing an institution. This might be called "self-directed orientation."

What kind of preparation is available for persons elected to the position? Over the years, the Association of Theological Schools has mounted various kinds of orientation programs for people who have been in office for two or three years. These programs ordinarily have been of two to four days duration. The Warren Deem Institute operated by the ATS with financial support from the Lilly Endowment from 1982 to 1990, was a four-week learning experience that dealt with many aspects of leadership and administration. With the exception of that institute, there has been no sustained orientation for presidents. There are a number of programs offered by universities through their schools of business management or education which are designed for new presidents of colleges and universities; some seminary presidents have attended these but find the contrast in numbers of students and faculty, relationships with government, research for business, and the size of staff available to the president to be so vastly different that the programs are not as valuable as one might hope.[5] So with the exception of the limited efforts of the ATS there is no specific orientation for seminary presidents.

What must be said, then, is that the majority—certainly not all—of the people who assume the responsibilities of a seminary presidency have little personal orientation to working with institutions. Candidates coming from outside the academy often fail to recognize that academic institutions have a unique life of their own. Nor can persons selected for these positions find a sustained training program to attend, even if their institutions had the monies to send them and they had the time to attend. As most presidents tell us, they had to learn everything while on the job. This is a systemic problem for higher education in general, not just for theological institutions, though it is probably more acute in the latter.

FACULTY

Robert Lynn has said that the faculty, *especially the faculty*, must re-evaluate its attitude toward the presidency.[6] Why the faculty? Having noted the faculty's role in governance, it is obvious there could be problems between the president and the faculty simply because of the complexity of shared governance. But, in addition, Leon Pacala has observed:

> There are ... faculty issues which are unique to our times and which render academic leadership quite problematic. The perennial tensions between faculty and administrative prerogatives are joined by new forms of inter-faculty conflicts, faculty versus church constituency oppositions, and faculty agendas that differ from and not infrequently impede presidential agendas.[7]

Pacala suggests there are two categories of reasons that cause faculty to "render academic leadership quite problematic." The first has to do with the "perennial tensions" between faculty and administration. One suspects that perennial tensions appear when the budget is being projected, when salary raises are announced, and when requests are made for faculty participation in the annual alumni/ae banquet. There is a sense in which this type of tension exists in every organization. One finds these tensions in a family as well as in the federal government.

But there are unique reasons why tensions exist between faculty and administration. First, we have noted that some faculty members believe the bureaucratic structures of administration skew, if not totally disrupt, the educational process. The end of administration is neatness, predictability, and efficiency. By contrast, the end of education is the formation of persons and the creation of new knowledge, neither of which lends itself to neatness, predictability, and efficiency. There is reason to believe that in respect to many administrative processes, the faculty may be right. There should, at least, be discussions about these matters, not just tensions.

The second underlying reason for perennial tensions is that faculty members as a group tend to think of administrative work as inferior to the kind of intellectual activity they practice.[8] We have noted that, in part at least, this is a failure to see the concreteness of the educational process. A third reason, which may incorporate the first two, is provided by William R. Brown; he contends that faculties have a culture as distinct as that of any foreign country.

> Few such solitary professions remain in our society today as that of the academician. Although he may reside in a large university and spend most of his time talking with or at others, the academician generally works alone. He prepares his own material, conducts his own courses, and evaluates his own students. The same singularity is present in much of his research. In this sense, academic performance is discrete. The academician is independent. The interdependence and division of labor that dominate relationships in a bureaucratic or industrial structure are not strong forces in academia. An understanding of academic politics begins with recognition of this distinction.[9]

Faculty members, trained to work in this solitary fashion, resist policies which by nature seek to regularize things they want left open; they chafe under teaching schedules and office hour requirements, since they want to control their own time; this, after all, is one of the benefits of being a professor. They are accustomed to debating the merits of any proposal from an infinite number of perspectives and thus find closure difficult; decisions are postponed for yet another meeting. They are, he argues, not well suited for the task of governance, even shared governance.

William Brown is not angry with faculty, but simply sees a serious problem between presidential efforts to organize and run an institution and the attitudes of the institution's chief citizens.[10]

But when Leon Pacala referred to faculty issues unique to our time that make the president's job difficult, he had other things in mind. For example, faculties in theological schools share the concern abroad in the churches and society that minority persons have been systematically excluded from such bodies as faculties. Thus, whenever there is a search for a new faculty member, many institutions will seek a woman or minority person qualified in the field. Search processes have become much more complex, especially in institutions where faculty members must belong to a given tradition. But there is an additional tension created when some contend that a candidate's qualification is enhanced by the very fact of being female or a person of color. Others seriously disagree. This discussion is further complicated by new canons of scholarship emerging from African-American Theology or Feminist Theology or Asian Theology or Gay and

Lesbian Theology. Since all theology creates the truths to which it points, these are not just variations on a theme. These are different "construals of the Christian thing." Therefore, when some members of a faculty object to the use of traditional rationality and argumentation as criteria for judging the adequacy of scholarship, the difficulty of even having a discussion is present. Seeking to do right can become divisive.

These are important issues. They lie at the very heart of the educational process, especially when ecclesiastical communities recognize their oneness with God's people throughout the world and the finiteness of all our perspectives. But seeking to recognize our pluralism raises basic questions of scholarship and truth.[11] For a president to preside over an institution caught up in these arguments, many of which are foreign to the very people the institution seeks to serve, is no easy task. The intellectual problems of searching for the truth, the perennial tensions between administrators and faculty, and the strange assumption that the educational process is somehow floating around unattached to the concrete realities of life and society make working with faculties tough.

Again, it should be underscored that these issues are and will be present in most theological schools regardless of who is president. They are matters that are built into the system of higher education in our time.

FUND RAISING

Historically, presidents have been expected to find support for their institutions. John Knox McLean argued in 1900 that "permanent" presidents were needed because of the fund raising demands of seminaries. Reading the histories of individual seminaries, one becomes aware of the endless search for financial support. Not only must support be found, but finding it is complicated and difficult for seminary presidents. Let me suggest a number of reasons for this.

1. During the past twenty-five or thirty years there have been many changes in ecclesiastical structures that have caused fund raising to resurface as a key issue, and a difficult one at that. Denominational mergers, as in the case of the United Church of Christ, left schools formerly supported by appropriations or gifts from judicatories without any support system for a season. When the two major Presbyterian bodies in the United States rejoined, a new system of support had to be developed since the former branches had different approaches. The Episcopal Church also developed

a new system; and many Roman Catholic seminaries that had depended on their orders or their bishops for support, have had to open development offices. Canadians seminaries have experienced similar disruption of the systems in the lessening of financial support by the government.

All of this must be understood in the context of the decline of giving in North America due to economic difficulties as well as other factors. These restructurings of ecclesial and political life have generated a tremendous growth in competition for funds. Thus the sociocultural context has exacerbated the Herculean task of fund raising for presidents.

2. Both faculty members and pastors, the sources of most new presidents, usually have little to do with money in their educational and professional experience. This point is related to the personal disposition or orientation of presidents mentioned previously. Religion—from the point of view of either faculty or pastors—is often thought of as a "noneconomic" force in our world. Pastors do not like to allude to money in sermons; they prefer that lay people manage the annual pledge solicitation. It is not uncommon to invite an outsider to preach on "pledge Sunday." Some confess to being uncomfortable around people who regularly handle large amounts of money or are themselves wealthy. Deeply buried in our consciousness lurks a notion that money—not the love of money, as the Scriptures suggest—is the root of all evil.

If this is true of many pastors, it is truer of faculty members, many of whom are ordained and live with similar feelings and ideas. Even more than pastors, they ordinarily have had little association with business executives and their world. It is not unusual to encounter persons in higher education who have developed an attitude of disdain for people who spend their lives making and investing money.[12] Sprinkled throughout the literature of higher education are concerns of faculty members, deploring the influence of trustees and administrators with their "business mentalities" in the affairs of education.[13] Presidents, in other words, come from contexts in which money, monied people, and the influence of the business community are not always viewed in a positive fashion. Yet the president is told to raise money, befriend monied people, and associate with leaders in the economic community.

3. Usually a president can count on graduates of the school to support it through large gifts, as well as linking her with others capable of making such gifts. But most graduates of seminaries enter church ministry, the teaching profession, or some other form of service-oriented employment, such as marriage counseling or prison chaplaincy. None of these is noted

for its high salary; no one gets rich pursuing these vocations. So unless graduates inherit money, they are not persons of great wealth.

It would seem, however, that they are well situated to lead presidents to persons able to give significantly. After all, church persons are noted for being the most generous people in our society. But many pastors hold the attitude toward money we have been discussing here. Some will frankly tell you they have no idea how much money anyone in their congregation has. They want to be careful not to favor persons with money as they visit and attend to other needs of the congregation. In addition, pastors are worried about their budgets and fear that members who give to a seminary may make smaller gifts to the local church. They hesitate, therefore, to assist presidents with their jobs.

While this attitude is not found among all clergy, it is prevalent. Fortunately, there are those who ably help presidents by arranging for meetings with potential givers. They see their actions as not only repaying the institution that educated them but also as serving the church through strengthening the theological enterprise.

4. Another group that traditionally assists the president in the task of fund raising is trustees. Theological institutions have traditionally had cadres of laypersons, frequently including trustees, who made the survival and growth of the institution possible by their generosity. Today many boards of trustees have clergy members and persons appointed by various judicatories who may or may not be very interested in theological education. Many of the laypersons on boards have only second-hand knowledge of theological education; they are likely to have attended college, but not a seminary. Strong loyalties may link them, and perhaps their parents and/ or children, to their alma mater, which in turn seeks their support. Loyalty to the seminary may be secondary. In addition, seminaries have tried to make sure that minorities and other under-represented persons sit on their boards so that these voices are not lost in forming policies for the education of clergy. They usually are not selected because of their ability to give money, but for much needed wisdom and insight. The composition of seminary boards is not always structured for fund raising.

Fortunately, many seminaries have extremely able and dedicated trustees who are willing to give generously and provide excellent help to the president in contacting others. But one must affirm that the board's role in the fund raising efforts of theological schools differs from that of many colleges or universities.

5. The lack of visibility of theological institutions is another factor in the development arena. Many people in churches attended a college or university as did their children, neighbors, and relatives; few, however, have any contact with a seminary. They know their pastor went to school to learn about "being a preacher," but they are not conversant with the school. In a recent study done by a major denomination in the United States, the number of church members who even knew the name of one seminary was very small.[14] Persons in leadership roles in denominations, including seminaries, are not well known within their constituencies as was once the case. When neither the school nor its president are known by the people who are supposed to support the institution, we should not be surprised to find fund raising difficult.

While giving to national church entities has declined, giving locally remains strong. Here again, visibility is a problem.

Leaders of eleemosynary institutions in local communities have a great advantage in fund raising over theological schools. The work of the latter is removed from the limelight of the community. What the seminaries do and how that affects the community is not always clear. Pastors may be on the boards of charitable organizations; they even may have founded such groups, but the average person does not know the formative impact of the seminary experience on the pastor. Centers for homeless children, the aging, or hospitals are seen and visited almost daily by persons in the community; retirement homes and hospice programs get the attention of donors quickly and unambiguously. For seminary presidents, on the other hand, the task of nurturing potential donors is time consuming since, in so many cases, one has to start "from scratch" to make the case for a seminary. The "good works" of a seminary are not self-evident.

6. Related to this lack of visibility is the hesitancy of foundations to give to theological schools. If the school bears the name of Roman Catholic or Baptist, foundations mention their fear of supporting sectarian institutions. To give to theological schools, they say, opens the door to criticism and for the other two or three hundred religious groups to ask to be treated equally. Some foundations may want evidence that theological schools contribute to the improvement of life in their community. Can one prove that educating clergy has had a beneficial effect on the larger society? If one does make such an argument, it is usually tentative and not supported by the "hard data" desired by foundation executives. The soup kitchen can report the number of hungry people they fed last week; the clinic can tell how many people they treated during the year; but the impact of theological

education is not so evident. This is not to say a case cannot be made; it is to recognize the difficulty of doing so.

Nevertheless, several major foundations in North America are not afraid to become involved in supporting religion, including theological education. There are also small family foundations in almost every community that have been very generous to seminaries, especially those located in the same community. Still, the percentage of support coming to seminaries from foundations remains small.

7. A final factor relates to the difficulty of securing and keeping good development officers. When a theological school advertises for such a person, salaries frequently prove to be a problem. Good development people can demand and get outstanding salaries compared with the staff compensation of most seminaries. It is sometimes possible to find a graduate of the school who has received or is willing to take training in this field. Such people can be invaluable. But most development staffs also need an attorney to deal with wills and bequests, the key to building endowments. Such highly trained persons are difficult to afford and keep, yet are desperately needed for doing adequate work in this age.

The list could go on and on. Some schools are limited as to what churches they can nurture. For example, some denominations have divided their constituencies into geographical sections and allow given institutions to work in only designated areas. Other churches will not let seminaries seek monies, except in very specific ways such as asking a church for a percentage of its annual operating budget. Faculties may have a more liberal mind-set than constituencies and thus their writings and speaking engagements may alienate prospective donors. And there are still sections of the church that believe seminaries are not necessarily good for pastors: they "take away the Spirit" and leave only a lot of learning.

Whether due to the attitudes toward money of many religious professionals (a theological matter), the institutional structures of denominations (an ecclesial issue), or the place of seminaries in the ecology of institutional life in North America (an environmental matter), fund raising is a problematic, systemic issue for presidents of theological schools.

This particular endemic problem is singled out by Leon Pacala:

> *The nature of theological school leadership is influenced by the requisites of financial development to a greater extent than any other single factor. They constitute a most significant criteria for the evaluation of candidates for presidential appointments. They are equally important in assessing the*

effectiveness of presidential leadership. They are also the grindstones that constantly wear down presidential energies, morale and self-confidence...[15]

STUDENTS

One final cluster of systemic problems presidents face centers in the students. First, there is the matter of recruitment. When things go well, as was the situation following World War II, seminaries do not worry about recruiting students; this was true for Catholics as well as Protestants. But when churches begin to talk about the "over supply" of clergy, the climate changes. When articles on this topic appear in *The New York Times* and *The Wall Street Journal*, people in general begin to take note. Before long, fewer and fewer people apply to seminaries. There is a variety of other reasons for the decline among the Catholics, but the results are the same. When Episcopal bishops and other church leaders refuse to endorse persons for the study of the ministry, there is little the seminary can do about the situation.

Do seminaries recruit? Do they try to persuade the few who are going to seminary to come to their schools as opposed to another institution in their tradition or an independent seminary? In most seminaries there is some ambiguity about recruiting. There are those who believe seminaries should do like colleges; that is, try to find people they can convince to join the student body. Others argue this is contrary to the calling of God. Since Roman Catholic candidates come either through their orders or are sent by bishops, there is little recruiting that can be done, except for laypersons, or the visiting of "sending bishops" on behalf of the school. Colleges and universities follow demographics and focus on persons graduating from high school. But since most seminarians do not come directly from baccalaureate study, demographics are not as useful a tool even if the relation between the call of God and recruiting activities of schools could be deduced.

Placement can be as much of a problem as recruiting. While theological schools in many traditions are not responsible for locating positions for their graduates, every school has some system for maintaining contact with judicatories or significant persons in the tradition to facilitate employment. But there are times when persons graduating from theological schools simply cannot find jobs. The administration of the school may realize that certain churches will not call females or gays and lesbians; they then have to counsel both prospective students and graduates that their chances of receiving a call to a congregation are slim. Older students, younger students, unmarried ones, minorities, and persons with handicaps also may require special attention in the placement process.

A president recently wrote of employing an enrollment manager. This is a new specialization widely used in colleges and universities that has to do with getting students, keeping them, and then assisting in their placement at graduation. The faculty was scandalized, believing the school had no business with "enrollment managers." In sum, the field of student enrollment is ambiguous at best. Many of the unique issues are related to the church systems of which the school is a part but does not control.

Second, let us look at the characteristics of the students who do come. One challenge presidents have these days is that many students come without any or much church background. They have become Christian, or even vaguely religious, through some small group or strictly personal experience. Thus they are enrolled in programs leading to ordination while knowing almost nothing about the church and its ministry. Many are the product of a "privatized" form of religion or Christianity which does not take seriously the community of faith or the life of the church. They want to fulfill their hunger for deeper religious experiences, but are not much interested in the theology and history of the people of God. This phenomenon is present among conservatives, Roman Catholics, and mainline seminaries. Catholics have devised a system whereby these candidates are required to live in one of their communities for a year or two before moving on to seminary. Many are required to do background study before entering priestly formation. Protestants do not have such a system.

There are also students who are filled with religious zeal. They are eager to enter active ministry and seminary is a necessary hoop to jump through along the way. They see no need to live in the seminary community; in fact, most have congregations which they serve while going to school. To get these students to study with seriousness can be a problem. Or, their religious zeal may come out in championing a social cause. They may rebel against such things as the administration's hiring policies or the firing of a staff member. In the 1960s, demands for new curricula nearly destroyed more than one school. Righteous indignation can fuel a conflagration in what is ordinarily a peaceful community. Few things are as difficult to deal with as a young, religious zealot! On the other hand, one president complained that students in his institution lacked zeal of any kind, save to impress church authorities and thus secure a good parish upon graduation.

He disliked the fact that they were "cookie cutter" members of his denomination.

Finally, I mention again the diversity of student bodies. In more recent times schools have experienced an influx of women, persons of color, gay and lesbian persons, internationals, and people who are handicapped, as well as large numbers of older students, referred to as "second career" students. As we noted in our review of history, seminaries have deliberately sought out persons to pursue a variety of special degree programs. Many of these persons are not "in residence," but commute from their homes. Extension schools may have their own campuses or share the facilities of a college many miles from the sponsoring institution. Thus there are amazing numbers of configurations of students. Each of these groups brings delightful contributions of variety, excitement, and gifts to the schools and to the ministry. But their presence calls upon seminaries to provide special course work, accessible housing, representation on the faculty and various committees, and additional financial aid. They also need counseling to assist them in tailoring the programs of the school to their special needs. If one operates an extension school, ways must be found to provide these resources.

Most seminaries want to be supportive of all these groups; they want to go beyond what the law requires, for example, with respect to handicapped persons. They want to adjust the curriculum for special groups, but there is only so much a small school with limited resources can do. The result is often tension which can be especially sharp when fueled by theological commitments.

When discussing students, the diverse nature of theological institutions becomes evident. The Orthodox Churches, the Roman Catholic Church, and others do not admit women to study for the priesthood. Other seminaries reflect the ethnicity of their denomination which has few, if any, minorities. This includes schools in the African-American traditions which have few whites enrolled in their student bodies. But most schools have had an influx of older, diverse students; this is due both to student choice of vocation and the multiplication of programs in seminaries. There is a sense in which the theological school exists for the sake of serving the students; but because of its hybrid nature, this service is not merely an academic matter but also a spiritual matter, a concern of the heart, a divine calling. Most theological schools were established to prepare persons for ordained ministry, but many are now engaged with a wide variety of students taking advantage of multiple programs. The student picture is complicated in many ways by the policies of the churches, the nature of the ministerial vocation, and the regulations of various groups—all beyond the control of the seminary.

CONCLUSION

My intention in this chapter has been to realistically adumbrate reasons people find the task of being president of a theological school difficult and to point out that many of these reasons are built into the systems that make theological education what it is. Presidents and trustees need to be aware of the existence of issues that are beyond the control of any person occupying the office. Simply knowing about some of these difficulties can help a president; being conscious of them can enable trustees to be more supportive and understanding.

One could take each of the rubrics used in this chapter to point to the joys that have come to presidents despite the inherent difficulties. Think of the lifelong friendships presidents have formed with students. Imagine the joy of enabling a faculty member to find the time and resources to publish a volume that will serve the cause of Christ for a generation. The companionship of trustees as a president struggles with difficult decisions creates bonds with people as few things can. It is a demanding life, but a rewarding one.

NOTES

[1] My good friend Barbara Wheeler, President of Auburn Seminary in New York, greatly objects to this construct. She believes the churches are so vastly different in their relationships with seminaries that to say they have an impact on the school could mean anything. It is also true that the academy is experienced quite differently by different institutions. The Berlin research model is strongly felt in some schools while the notions of *paideia* are constitutive of the life of others. President Wheeler also points out that seminaries are civil institutions, having state charters to offer degrees, having personnel laws to obey, and all the rest. Why not use this rather than church?

While I appreciate her concern enough to note it here, I think the construct of hybrid institution, the blending of church and academy, is a useful one.

[2] Professor Kelsey's book, *To Understand God Truly*, elaborates on how the various "construals" of the faith affects seminaries, especially Chapter 2.

[3] See Note 7 of Chapter 1 for a listing of some of the contributors to the dialogue.

[4] Kelsey, *To Understand God Truly*, 182-187.

[5] In an interesting and helpful publication for new presidents of colleges and universities, there is a list of programs for new presidents sponsored by a variety of groups, 43ff. Actually this small booklet has some very helpful articles which could be useful for new presidents of theological schools. Estela M. Bensimon, Marian L. Gade, and Joseph F. Kauffman, *On Assuming a College or University Presidency: Lessons and Advice from the Field* (Washington: American Association for Higher Education,1989).

[6] Lynn, "Coming Over the Horizon" in *Good Stewardship*, 55.

[7] Op. cit. 24.

[8] Katarina Schuth observes that within Roman Catholic schools the rector's job is made more difficult by faculty not "understanding the importance of administration in general, and as a result failing to cooperate with or appreciate the person in leadership." 89-90, *Reason for the Hope: The Future of the Roman Catholic Theologates.*

[9] *Academic Politics*, 10-11.

[10] Ibid., 8. Brown believes that the two perspectives, that of administrative work and academic work, need to mesh together or at least the president must understand both and be able to fit them together.

[11] Max L. Stackhouse addresses these issues in *Apologia: Contextualization, Globalization, and Mission in Theological Education* (Grand Rapids: Eerdmanns, 1988). A Roman Catholic scholar, Fr. Robert J. Schreiter deals with similar issues in *Constructing Local Theologies* (Maryknoll, NY: Orbis Books, 1986). See also F. Clark Power and Daniel K. Lapsley, editors,*The Challenge of Pluralism: Education, Politics, and Values*(Notre Dame: University of Notre Dame Press, 1992).

[12] Robert Wuthnow is doing research on this strange attitude of Christians toward money which has a bearing on my argument. See his article, "Pious materialism: How Americans view faith and money." *Christian Century.* Mar.3,1993 (Vol.110,No.7), 238-42.

[13] Thorstein Veblen, *The Higher Learning in America* (New York: Sagamore Press, 1957). This is reprinted from the original 1918 book. Veblen is not only alarmed by the presence of the "captains of industry" but wants to label presidents as "captains of erudition." There are few if any books written in the past fifty years on the operation of universities

that do not quote from Veblen. In more recent times, Robert Bellah and his colleagues have lashed out at the notion of the university as being "market-driven," that is, supplying graduates with a way to make a living or training people for industry alone. They believe these people reject the university as a community of moral discourse. In this type of discussion, it appears to me that people frequently confuse efforts to calculate the cost of this or that program with the changing of the basic purpose of the university. Even in a community of moral discourse, someone has to be responsible, morally responsible, for the proper use of funds provided either by the state or individuals. In recent times, several major universities have been accused of misusing funds. See Bellah *et al, The Good Society* (New York: Alfred A. Knopf,1991), 169-70.

[14] The General Assembly Special Committee to Study Theological Institutions (Draft Report) April 1992, Presbyterian Church (USA). Based on a survey done by the Presbyterian Panel, the study discovered that most laypersons and some clergy are unfamiliar with the Presbyterian theological institutions. Though most clergy could claim to know one or two of the schools fairly well, no more than five percent of laity could make the same claim, 39.

[15] Leon Pacala, op. cit., 24. Italics are his.

8

STEWARDS OF HOPE

In addition to carefully listing many of the realities that make the presidency difficult, I must go on to say that these are only part of the challenge. In my opinion there is probably no more exciting position in the church of today and tomorrow than that of the presidency of a theological institution. I believe the position holds great promise and opportunity for faithfulness to the Gospel and the future of the church. Just as the president is uniquely situated within the theological community to exert considerable influence, so the presidency of a theological institution is strategically located within the life of the denominations to enable the person in the office to lead the larger community in significant ways.

By its very nature, the office calls upon the occupant to be a steward of the past, to keep alive the history of the school within its tradition and larger community. The office calls upon the president to dream about and plan for the future; thus the president is a steward of hope, not only for the institution, but also for the larger community of faith which has commitments that press it to be concerned for the whole world. The position clearly demands that the occupant be a faithful steward of the resources of the institution for the present as well as for the future.

Such statements may seem strange in light of the fact that I have affirmed throughout this book that there is no such thing as *the* presidency, only many particular presidents occupying positions that greatly vary. But my analysis of conversations with and documents written by presidents in numerous traditions covering a significant period of time, has led me to affirm that there is some commonality among the various positions. This analysis delineates certain factors that tend to be present regardless of the location of the office. I have, for example, insisted that any presidency is shaped by the intersection of a number of forces. As we begin our thinking about the future of the office, let me summarize by identifying the important components of any presidency so we can more adequately reflect on the presidency of a particular institution.

DIMENSIONS OF THE OFFICE

How can one think about a particular presidency? How can trustees analyze the job when seeking to call someone to fill it? How can candidates understand what it will mean to be president of a seminary in the years ahead? How do people now in the office analyze the swirling chaos around them in order to think and plan about the future? To simplify this task I propose clusters of items which I refer to as dimensions of the office.

There are four major categories or dimensions. First, is the *environment*—the sociocultural setting—which includes the mood of the nation, demographics, economic climate, and the dominant organizational patterns of the time, and geographic location. Clark Kerr and Marian Gade use the rubric of historical contexts—the external and internal environments—to deal with these matters.[1] Their grouping of external and internal environments together is understandable, since the internal conditions of the Berkeley campus, for example, during the 1960s and 1970s was clearly a reflection of the "external" environment (the Vietnam War and the mood of disaffection from American institutions in general). The same can be said about dominant organizational models of any period. They will be reflected in the churches as well as the seminaries themselves. Economic conditions in the country will determine to a large extent the economic health of an individual school. Factors in the host culture that significantly affect a school must always be considered.

While the external sociocultural environment has an impact on the internal affairs of the school, the second dimension is specifically an internal environment. It relates to matters involving ecclesiastical *tradition*, campus ethos, and the cycle of an institution's life. In any school, its particular "construal" of the Christian faith, to use Kelsey's language, carries a tradition that shapes its goals and curriculum, along with its academic, spiritual, and common life. In addition, the composition and powers of the board, the method of selecting trustees, and the stated purpose of the institution are affected by its relationship with the church. Clearly, selection of faculty, the place of worship in the community, emphases such as academic freedom, and concern with evangelism and/or social action reflect the church tradition as well as the ethos of a school. Ecclesial traditions influence the character of a school, even those which are "interdenominational" or "nondenominational" or related to universities.

The third category consists of specific *practices* expected of the president. In addition to being an administrator, is he or she expected to be "dean of the chapel," to set the tone and style of worship for the community? Does the financial situation demand a great emphasis on fund raising, or are funds provided by another institution? Is the president expected to be active in many of the structures of the denomination? What kind of direct authority is over the president, dictating major investments of time and energy? While all presidents engage in some form of administrative activity, other practices are influenced by the tradition, environment, and cycle of the school's life.

The fourth dimension is the *person* of the president. An individual's character, style, previous training and experience, faith, and family situation contribute to shaping the presidency, as does the support provided by trustees and others. Along with these factors is the degree to which a president identifies with the school's tradition and how much familiarity he has with its ethos. In addition, each person brings to the job varying gifts and abilities which will be tested in an environment where passionate beliefs and opinions are routine. For instance, a president must be able to listen to the institution's various constituencies and then shape those strong, yet particularized dreams into a clear vision which remains faithful to the school's purpose. Beyond all this, his understanding of the nature of shared governance, the mind-set of the faculty, dynamics within the board of trustees, and his own day-to-day style of leadership obviously will affect the character of his presidency.

These categories are not discrete; they flow back and forth into one another. The organizational model prominent in a society is likely to affect the ecclesiastical structure of the supporting churches as well as the seminary. In other words, environment and tradition are not independent of each other. The person who has taken vows of obedience may relate to church authorities differently than someone in the free church tradition; the person and tradition interact. In times of economic recession, the practice of fund raising may demand more attention and consume more energy than at other times; thus the environment influences practices, which are in turn colored by the president's personality and style as she works in accordance with ecclesial guidelines for fund raising and a host of other things. Environment contributes to shaping the person as much as tradition and practices; tradition and ethos interact with practices as much as the environment. At the intersection of these forces, stands the president.

No simple listing of components can provide an exact description of any presidency. It does, however, provide us with categories for thinking about the office. What are the environmental factors that most presidents must deal with today? At the time of this writing the climate is right for organizations to become leaner. Why? Because, in part, state colleges and universities are down-sizing as well as raising fees; the government has cut back on student aid; churches are reducing support. In short, presidents may be pushed by economics and the environment to consider retrenchment. Yet another environmental factor is that with each new federal administration come inevitable changes in legal requirements that may affect everything from accommodations for handicapped persons to regulations for charitable giving and accounting procedures. What is happening in these areas today?

What about the ecclesial tradition of the institution in this era? Have the "national bodies" assumed more control over their institutions or less? What are denominational pressures for the merger of institutions, redefining their purposes, and for cooperation with other schools? What requirements has the national body placed on fund raising or where its students may attend seminary? Does the denomination and the ethos of the school allow gay and lesbian persons to be called to the faculty? How much does a particular church tradition affect the content of the courses?

What practices or activities does the office require at this juncture of the institution's life? Is there a serious need for organizing and regularizing internal procedures? In what areas does the board need educating? Are there faculty and staff who must be asked to leave? What aspects of the personality and training of the president are going to be important in the coming days? Does he need to understand the faculty better? Are her skills in the financial area adequate? How much longer does the president plan to stay before retiring?

The perspective of this book stresses how much the office of the president is shaped by the world and the tradition, or the expression of the church that dominates the school. In addition, there are other institutions—which I shall define shortly—that greatly influence seminaries and press them with new demands. In the remainder of this chapter I will discuss some of these sociocultural factors as well as ecclesiastical realities that I consider to be significant as we think about the presidency in the future. The office and, indeed, the schools, must be seen and dealt with in their contexts. We no longer have the luxury of thinking about theological seminaries in isolation from these other factors. Seeing the theological school and its presidency in *context* is a matter that must be faced by trustees, presidents, and candidates for the office.

Neither can we merely keep the theological school operating day to day; we must plan for the future. As Robert Wuthnow reminds us, we are not so much trying to forecast the future, but

> to consider the challenges ahead, asking about the direction of present trends, looking at what we have and what we want, and then by considering the future, assess better where our present energies should lie.[2]

It is to some of these present trends that we now turn.

INTERLOCKING INSTITUTIONS

By saying the seminary must be seen in its context, I am suggesting it is an institution which is related to other institutions of our society and especially ecclesiastical ones. It is related to these other institutions and must be understood in that context. After years of neglect, discussions of institutions—their nature and characteristics—are becoming more commonplace in our society.[3] We are perhaps more aware today than ever of the many institutions to which seminaries have been related over the years. Seminaries grew and matured as part of an interlocking network of institutions.[4] The home once consciously nurtured the Christian faith; the church and its beliefs were valued both by the home and the community. Early public schools were little more than extensions of the church school in the sense of reinforcing Christian faith, primarily the Protestant ethos. There were church- related colleges with required worship and Bible courses. Graduates of these institutions frequently went on to seminary, the final and highest piece in this educational construct.

While no doubt I am romanticizing the past to make a point, it is true that such a network in some form did exist. Much of this is now gone. There are fragments here and there, but there is no network of nurturing educational institutions which children of the church learn about and experience as an ordinary part of church life. Furthermore, many seminary students in our time do not "grow up" in the church, with or without this network. In instances where interlocking institutions do remain intact, seminaries move along in much the same way they did decades ago.

This is the situation in several smaller denominations, which function almost like large, extended families; where there are still parochial schools for the children and even church-related colleges of the same denomination. They maintain a supporting ecological system. Recruiting students, finding operating funds, calling faculty are all supported by this system. But in most other settings, seminaries are left more or less by themselves.

A similar scenario could be given for Roman Catholic institutions. In many areas, the parochial school system is gone. The preparatory schools, called minor seminaries, which prepared students for theological studies are gone or greatly diminished. Consequently, one Catholic rector says their former type of theological seminary is a thing of the past. Gone is the institution located in a diocese, supported by a bishop who also sent students, staffed with laypersons from religious orders, and whose faculty was composed of priests. Lack of students, the demise of many orders, a shortage of qualified teachers, and the financial crunch has caused many preparatory schools and smaller theological seminaries to close. Some have merged, or entered a consortium, but even these solutions have their problems. The institutions which, in Catholic tradition, made theological seminaries possible are greatly diminished.

A few church groups are trying to turn back the clock by establishing closely-knit families and operating kindergartens through twelfth grade schools, and even colleges. A few "megachurches" are establishing their own seminaries. But these are isolated communities; they are not in the mainstream. David F. Wells, an evangelical spokesperson, believes these folk do not realize that the culture in which they live has permeated them and their values, even in the way they conceive of the substance and purpose of the Christian faith. Thus, strong tides of our secular culture infuse the very people who imagine they are going against "secular humanism" and other modern plagues.[5] But if they are unaware of the institutions which are shaping them, they still must be given credit for attempting to build supporting institutions which they hope will form their future and that of the nation. Despite these few efforts, the network of institutions which traditionally has supported theological schools is in poor repair.

On the other hand, Robert Bellah and Christopher Adams note in a recent article that there is a revival of interest in academic circles concerning institutions and their nurture.[6] They also list a number of experiments in towns and cities designed to create and strengthen institutions.[7] If there is research, followed by articles and books as well as models about preserving, creating, and renewing institutions, then presidents who are educators may have access to the necessary tools to learn to think and work systemically. Since it is no longer possible to think about their schools and their futures in isolation from the institutions that make seminary existence possible, they must begin to address the role that theological schools might play in re-establishing institutions or creating new ones that will strengthen the life of the churches and contribute to the survival of seminaries.

There are examples of this happening in our time. The president and certain faculty at Louisville Presbyterian Theological Seminary were instrumental in finding funds for and producing a series of studies to help Presbyterians understand their past and reflect on their future. Such a study assists in recovery of identity by pointing to institutions that have had constructive influences within the denomination. More recently, the dean of a Methodist institution, together with a church historian has projected a major study of that denomination and its relationship to American society with the same purposes in mind. In one small denomination the seminary faculty is invited to attend every national meeting of the governing body and encouraged to engage in debates and discussions of issues that come before the church. This particular denominational structure encourages the possibility of theological reflection in these meetings. This may be a step in the direction of re-establishing the value of theological dialogue in the life of the church. It clearly highlights the importance this denomination attributes to its theological faculties. Depending on polity and tradition, there surely are numerous other illustrations of what can be done. These hopeful signs relate to what Ann Swidler, one of Bellah's colleagues, asserts about the need to renew institutions that contribute to the moral foundations of such organizations as theological schools.[8]

While reference has been made to the several institutions that once formed a support system for the seminaries, it should be noted that this system was not the result of an organized plan; seminary presidents and denominational leaders did not create such a support system "on purpose." It simply arose out of the give and take of life during the early nineteenth century. I suggest that one of the primary tasks that presidents of seminaries and denominational leaders have in the coming days is to envision new or revived institutions which will help give unity and support to the people of God in our time. What kind of networking institutions can be built in our time, perhaps using the technology so readily available to all? Can new

systems be projected, nurtured, and encouraged by the seminaries working
with others in the church structures?

OTHER INSTITUTIONS

Reference was made previously to theological reflection taking place
in meetings of the courts of a particular denomination. This "institution,"
this shared value, this pattern of behavior was singled out because many
believe it has collapsed or disappeared. We might even say that theology
itself is no longer valued. Writing as a spokesperson for "mainline" churches,
John B. Cobb, Jr., a distinguished theologian and long-time seminary
professor, argues that

> Theology as the serious activity of faith seeking understanding or self-
> conscious Christian reflection on important issues has disappeared from
> many churches. While some members of these churches still engage in
> theological reflection, theology no longer plays an important role in the
> church's life. It exists on the periphery, tolerated but not employed in
> making basic decisions.[9]

Cobb says he is talking about mainline churches, not the evangelical
tradition in America. But, as we have seen, David Wells says that
evangelicals have done the same thing.[10] He is as concerned as Cobb that
Christians do not even try to think theologically, nor do they care about
theology.

Both Cobb and Wells argue that theology, which can give integrity to
both life and thought in the church, is no longer valued either by the church
or the seminary. The latter is intent upon graduating persons who provide
congregations with the type of leaders they desire; this does not always
include being able to think theologically or to help others engage in this
practice.

But the writings of such people as Cobb and Wells have engendered
something of a revival in theological dialogue. There is reason to hope for
the renewal of this vital institution so closely related to theological schools.
What are the things a theological school might do within its own structure
as well as in cooperation with other ecclesiastical institutions to promote
the theological dialogue so vital to the health of the church?

Another illustration of deteriorating institutions is the weakening, if
not collapse, of denominations themselves. Much has been written about
this matter in recent years. Sociologist Robert Wuthnow documents the

decline of denominations in his studies. There are many reasons for this, such as the mobility of the population, the disaffection with leadership of the denominations, and the "privatizing" of religion. The result is fairly clear; people look for congregations near their homes, made up of people like themselves, who agree with them on social issues—such as homosexuality or abortion. The great ecclesiastical traditions are no longer deeply rooted in our consciousness.

The collapse of denominations with their theological traditions has many ramifications. The loss of a sense of ownership for denominational institutions like seminaries is one of the most obvious. A recent study reveals that few laypersons even know the names of their schools. Many pastors of mainline denominations did not attend their denominational schools and are therefore not socialized into the ethos of their traditions. This applies to most mainline denominations, with the exception perhaps of Lutherans.[11] During the Vietnam War, I recall asking a trustee of a certain institution, "Why do you remain on this board? You disagree with everything the seminary stands for." He replied, "Well, the school is a bastard, but it is our bastard and we'll support it." This kind of loyalty and willingness to stick with an institution, even in the midst of profound disagreement, is gone.

The other side of this coin is that despite all that has been said, many seminaries show considerable signs of strength within the denominational systems that remain. Seminaries are one of the few institutions of the church that survive, and some of these are more or less intact. There may be underlying reasons for this. For example, in the context of setting goals for a capital campaign several years ago, a survey was made among members of the United Church of Christ asking them to identify their primary concerns for their church. The first priority people gave was for well-prepared pastors. Deeply rooted in the hearts of many church folk, regardless of denominational background, may be a serious desire for adequate leadership in congregations and larger church bodies. Some might argue that these findings reflect the low opinion of church leaders in our time, but nevertheless, the survey indicated that people value good church leadership. Theological schools may, therefore, have more of an entree with the church public than any other ecclesiastical institution.

The study done by Clark Roof for this project indicates that leaders in the denominations still think highly of seminary presidents and call upon them for advice from time to time. They may not have the clout they once had, but compared to other leaders, they do not come off badly. In the smaller, more conservative denominations, seminary presidents are thought of as charismatic leaders, highly respected and valued. The point is that seminaries and their leaders are not starting at ground zero in seeking to build new alliances within church structures.

The success of independent seminaries may point to the possibility of finding persons willing to support and care for a particular type of education. President Robert Cooley of Gordon-Conwell Theological Seminary refers to the "publics" who support the type of education that a school provides. They are persons from a large number of denominations or independent settings who want the education themselves or want their pastors to experience that distinctive type of education. The growth of Fuller Theological Seminary, Asbury, and others clearly reflects the same thing. Networks, systems of support, and caring can be constructed.

This may mean seminaries can be centers of renewal for denominations. Robert Wuthnow uses an interesting illustration when he suggests that being Christian is like being an American. But it is probably more interesting and helpful if we are also Americans who are Southerners, or New Yorkers, or Midwesterners. Denominations are like these regions; they refine and color our citizenship, our Christianity.[12] Wuthnow also observes that

> it does seem to me that confessional traditions also make continuing sense: they will remain important considerations to the definition of religious institutions and to the lives of individuals of faith, and they will inform the perspectives of academicians as well.[13]

Seminaries may be able to help denominations learn to tell their stories, emphasize their heritages, and cherish their symbols without reviving the denominational pettiness and competition of earlier days. Seminaries even may be able to model in their lives together the value of such institutions as denominations and the concomitant theological reflection. But these institutions will have to be very clear about their purposes and offer distinctive educational options.[14]

THE POSTMODERN WORLD

In an interesting book on using the imagination in interpreting Scripture, Walter Brueggemann, a longtime member of the seminary community, argues that what modern persons have accepted as "reality,"— the views of economics, politics, and even science—is perceived today as merely human construal, much of which is proving inadequate for present-day life. The ways in which we think, feel, and respond to our environment are no longer seen as fixed and determined by previous points of view. This recognition of the social construction of reality enables us to operate in a new epistemological context: how we know and what we can know is no longer determined simply by a limited scientific outlook on reality. In this setting, theologians can neither pretend to be privileged insiders, having "the straight word from God," nor can they be excluded as outsiders, persons trivialized by the intellectuals of our time. Brueggemann affirms that our Christian faith, "our memory in faith," provides materials out of which an alternatively construed world can be imagined and proposed.[15] Thus, we are entering an era in which creative interpretations of the Scriptures might well provide for us a new world view and lead to imaginative forms of ministry.

Many others agree with Brueggemann. David Ray Griffin, who wrote for and edited the book, *Spirituality and Society*, offers some exceptional insights into our postmodern world.[16] While not every approach to the postmodern scene is viewed as positive by Griffin and his colleagues, certainly the flexibility that the new options are offering is being welcomed in the academy as well as the church. In an interview for this project, President Thomas Gillespie of Princeton Theological Seminary, stated that he believes the intellectual excitement created by this new situation can provide the incentive for a new wave of creative theological and biblical scholarship. The possibilities of envisioning new forms of congregational ministry are just beginning. Such visions could emanate from seminaries.

One must acknowledge that the intellectual leadership in the religious world, including the world of biblical scholarship, has shifted over the years from the seminaries to the university departments of religion. This is not to say that seminary faculties have not generated scholarly artifacts in recent years; it simply recognizes that they have been overshadowed for a variety of reasons. I list the new challenge here because one can hope that presidents and faculties of theological institutions will deliberately set their minds to fulfill the agenda sketched for us by Brueggemann. The church's engagement with the intellectual community is not an easy one—as Douglas Sloan delineates in his new book, *Faith and Knowledge*.[17] It is nevertheless, an exciting possibility.

OTHER IMPORTANT TASKS

While lacking the glamour of some of the previously mentioned opportunities, there are a number of areas that most theological schools could tackle that may provide leadership for the churches and hope for their own future. An arena for learning to think and work systemically has been created by denominational mergers, along with the decline of denominational membership and funding. Both of these changes have raised afresh the question of the number of seminaries owned or related to a given denomination. Some face this issue by suggesting seminary presidents continue to do what they have been doing, but do more of it faster. This will not solve the problem for the denomination nor ultimately for the school.

How should these situations be faced? There is a tendency among some to want a national body to determine policy and even the survival of theological institutions. Moving the fate of seminaries into the hands of a denominational committee or group, *may* run the risk of having crucial decisions made by persons who are unaware of the historic roots, support, and influence of these institutions. Many fear that such committees might push for uniformity in standards for admission and graduation which will eliminate the most creative students. But in other situations uniform standards may raise the level of ministry and should not automatically be dropped. What can be done to ensure that such committees do not fall into simple solutions to complex problems? The answer resides with the particular structure and governance of individual denominations or traditions. Presidents and trustees need to be active in any denominational moves, not simply to argue for the survival of their institutions, but to contribute to the health of the larger body by imaginatively considering alternatives. Maybe someone ought to ask: How many and what kind of seminaries would this church need if there were to be a surge of new members?

Persons need to be present on such occasions in order to ask other questions as, "What can these unique institutions contribute to the health and well-being of the larger church?" The answer may lie in the area of closure or merger with other institutions. But it might equally reside in encouraging theological institutions to find a calling unique to our age and the needs of the church at this juncture; or it may result in the conviction that nothing is needed more at the moment than well-prepared persons for leadership in the church.

In the final analysis, it may be that presidents and trustees have to take the initiative in raising the question of survival for their particular schools, facing the possibility of merger or the moving into a consortium of schools. There is a long history of attempts to close seminaries and the record is dismal; most are still there even after exhaustive studies and many proposals. Presidents have hesitated to deal with this because they do not want their institutions to disappear while they are serving. Closing a group of seminaries to establish two or three new ones runs the risk of having little support for the new institutions. The attitude of constituents may be, "It's not ours; it belongs to somebody else."

So whether dealing with the issues of too many seminaries, or with the problems of nurturing healthy denominationalism, educator/presidents and trustees are going to have to deal with the *system* of which they are a part.

The foregoing makes it clear that the matter of the clarification or renewal of the institution's basic purpose is of prime importance. This has been emphasized throughout the book. The literature is available, the dialogue is in process. The president needs to engage the board and faculty in this ongoing discussion. Should theological institutions change their reason for existence and seek to make some new contribution to the church other than preparing persons for ordained ministry? Where a denomination has too many theological schools this is certainly a question that cannot be avoided.

Another opportunity for seminaries to lead resides in the question of governance of educational institutions. Maybe one should say *questions* about governance, since there are clearly several. There has been a great deal of experimentation with creating, operating, and strengthening boards of trustees. The Catholic schools have been working at this for some twenty years in efforts to combine their polity with effective boards. Some Canadian schools are now experimenting with alternate board structures. Many Protestant schools have seen the membership and nature of their boards shift with denominational mergers and funding patterns. Foundations have encouraged strong boards through a variety of programs. What is the best board structure for theological schools? Does each board need to reflect the nature of the church governance of which the school is a part? Can seminaries model good governance as a part of their teaching ministry?

A second question relates to "shared governance." Studies, some of which I have mentioned in this book, indicate that the current form of governance is cumbersome. While many of us think it can be made to work, the question remains as to whether it should. Are seminary trustees, faculties, and administrations secure enough and trusting enough of one another to experiment with new forms?

To accomplish this goal, faculty members will have to examine carefully their commitments to academic guilds. As has been indicated, these groups of scholars bring a healthy influence to theological faculty members by keeping them in the mainstream of scholarship. God seldom has been served by ignorance. But when the perspectives of the guilds determine faculty areas of interest and research, the church's faith and mission is often neglected.

David Kelsey argues that academic disciplines in theological education be shaped by a concern for the role of the particular subject matters in the life of Christian congregations which are engaged in responding to the Gospel as they understand it. What role does the Bible have in nurturing faith? What does the sociology of religion tell us about the presence and use of power within a congregation and its larger community? How has the practice of worship been distorted over the years? Kelsey's suggestion has merit in my opinion.[18]

If theological faculty members were to adopt such a proposal, it is possible they could remain active in their guilds and yet bring a distinctive perspective which would make a contribution to those guilds. Their scholarly work would more adequately reflect their vocations as members of a theological school faculty.[19] This is clearly the type of educational challenge faced by presidents and faculties in the days ahead.

Still another challenge relates to the cost of theological education. Have we priced ourselves out of the market with a form of education that is too expensive for the church to bear? With the professionalization of faculty, seminaries (like universities) have developed elaborate forms of specialized courses and learning experiences. We already have seen the enormous increase in administrative cost over the years; this is related to educational costs as well as demands from outside the institution. Computers and other technological wonders hold the promise of smaller staffs and less overhead; but for most, this remains in the realm of fiction.

I am not attempting to blame any single group for the high cost of theological education, so much as to raise the question of the expense of the entire system. If we do not return to "mom and pop" operations—and I doubt the various laws of the land and professional guilds would let us— and if we are not to use antiquated or mechanized forms of education, is there nothing we can do?

I wish I had an answer to my own question. One alternative appears to be to continue to live with the impact of the entrepreneurial spirit upon the schools—which may be having serious adverse effects. Both faculty and presidents believe they must find new markets, create new programs, offer new services if they are to endure. While most of us would agree with the motivation of serving God's people in a variety of ways, a theological school can lose its soul in trying to survive by doing all things for all people. Another alternative appears to be replacing teachers with programmed, computerized courses; the long range effects of this process on education is frightening.

In this section I have suggested a number of areas for reflection. No one knows what the future holds, but presidents need to be persons who plan, not simply individuals who try to preserve what they inherited. Preserving the best from the past may indeed be a high calling for a president, but this should be done as part of the overall planning for the future of the school.

CONCLUDING WORD

At one point in the process of writing this book I considered calling it *Stewards of Hope: A Study of the Seminary Presidency.* My reasoning was that presidents of theological institutions are in unique positions during this particular era to offer encouragement to the churches and society. Helping the churches rediscover their historic roots and traditions, offering new models of governance both for the church and academy, probing a realignment of the academic disciplines so they can contribute more directly to the life of the people of God, becoming instrumental in establishing new institutions or in reviving old ones that will strengthen the life of the church, demonstrating that much can be accomplished with limited resources, preparing persons more adequately for ministerial leadership, using creatively the resources entrusted to them—these are but a few of the possibilities one can envision for future presidents. These educator/presidents may indeed be stewards of hope, though the task is not, and will not, be easy.

I am confident that my characterization of the president as a teacher/educator will not be well received by some. Defining the office in this manner takes away part of the glamour associated with leaders, with corporate executives in our society. Yet the notion of the president as first among equals in the educational arena might help bring educational questions into the foreground of the seminary's life; it might do much to heal the wounds that have been created between administration and faculty; it might change the "texture" of life within the institution. The president who shares uniquely in the life of the many segments of the seminary has the possibility of being the pivotal educator. While not denigrating CEOs, I propose that the educator should be profoundly valued in the academic community as well as in the church.

Some will no doubt object that in a day when academic roles, status, and basic identity are determined by subject matter, the president as educator would appear to have no distinctive area of expertise and no distinctive role. This reminds me of the story told by Mark R. Schwehn in *Exile from Eden*. While participating in a scholarly discussion group in the Chicago area, the members—all part of some university faculty—were requested to state their occupations as they had listed them on their tax returns in order to introduce themselves and fill a little time while waiting for latecomers. Moving briskly around the room, people responded, "sociologist," "anthropologist," "historian," "psychologist." Schwehn's response was "college teacher." The reaction of others was "a combination of mild alarm and studied astonishment." [20] Schwehn's occupation was that of a *teacher* who was also a highly trained historian. There may be something amiss about a faculty member's identification of herself with her discipline.

As faculty members might first think of themselves as teachers, so I believe it is altogether appropriate for the president to think of his calling as that of an educator. Plato, Whitehead, Dewey and a host of others considered education a worthy subject for reflection and writing. There is no lack of scholarly material from the past to say nothing of the contributions of those who have worked as educators in our time. We should not be embarrassed by lack of subject matter. The president should be defined by what she is engaged in doing, just as a faculty member is defined as a teacher.

Again, some will argue that everyone involved in theological education could define themselves as educators. The director of buildings and grounds, for example, might declare himself an educator. There is a sense in which such a person along with the chef, the secretaries, and the receptionist are sharing in the educational process taking place in the institution. But one could hardly say that these persons are primarily about the task of designing learning experiences. The director of buildings and grounds may in fact design a learning experience for his staff from time to time, if he is a good director, but to imagine that he would devote his time to this in the same way that faculty members and presidents do is a bit farfetched. But for such persons to see themselves on an educational continuum is not a bad thing, either for them or for the president.

The big fear is that this conceptualization of the office will enable presidents to simply keep on doing what they are doing, but to feel better about it. That in itself is not necessarily bad, but if the conceptualization encourages presidents to consider in concert with others, for example, the educational implications of what the introduction of computers into the classroom or in place of classroom means—so much the better. If this perception of the office encourages presidents to reflect on what the unique history of their institution within a denomination or tradition means for the educational task of the church in the years ahead, then the conceptualization is a good one. While there is no magic involved, this proposed way of viewing the office can encourage the sharing of educational questions with the dean, trustees, faculty, and administration.

The view of the presidency offered here and the leadership style of the educator/president reflects the changes in our society, some of which have been noted in this study. There was an era when presidents were noted for their *power*; they could make major decisions and shape institutions almost by themselves. In our time, people in executive positions realize that they use *influence* not power. This is not to suggest that presidents have no power, for they do. But it is to propose that defining the primary thrust of the position in terms of influence fits our current situation more adequately.

I believe this concept of leadership is consistent with the nature of education, as well as with the pattern of ministry which Christ modeled in serving rather than being served. Thus presidents, like all educators, will be constantly learning from those around them and using their own gifts to persuade others to follow the One whom the community seeks to obey.

The difficulties of the task will not go away; they are embedded in the structures of the church and the world of which the seminary is a part. But being conscious of the difficult areas, seeing them as part of the larger picture, might well enable presidents, trustees, and faculty to deal more adequately with these challenges in the years ahead. We can pray that the seriousness of the task will encourage key members of the theological community to work in concert with their counterparts in kindred institutions for the sake of the church.

A primary calling of the educator/president is to remind the seminary community of its roots, the narratives—including biblical narratives—that are constitutive for the life of the school and the church. The president must take the initiative in clarifying the purpose of the school in the economy of God, and lead the way in living out the hope that is both personal and institutional. Hope, after all, is a gift of God. And the Gospel makes us all stewards of hope.

NOTES

[1] Clark Kerr and Marian Gade, *The Many Lives of Academic Presidents: Time, Place and Character*, 79ff.

[2] *Christianity in the 21st Century*, 4.

[3] See, for example, Robert Bellah, Richard Madsen, William Sullivan, Ann Swidler, Steven Tipton, *The Good Society*,(New York: Alfred A. Knopf, 1991).

[4] Robert Lynn wrote about this phenomenon and often spoke about it more than twenty-five years ago; it has become part of our intellectual furniture. He ably shows the affects of a supporting ecology for the Sunday School movement as well as what happens when the system breaks down. See Robert W. Lynn and Elliott Wright, *The Big Little School* (Nashville: Abingdon, 1980), 146ff. Earlier he wrote about the same in *Protestant Strategies in Education* (New York: Association Press, 1964).

[5] David F. Wells, *No Place for Truth: Or, Whatever Happened to Evangelical Theology?*

[6] "Strong institutions, good city." by Robert N. Bellah and Christopher Freeman Adams. *The Christian Century*. June 15-22, 1994. Vol.111,No.19, 604-607. The other books by Bellah and his colleagues that have been mentioned deal with this subject in greater detail, especially *The Good Society*.

[7] Bellah and Adams, op. cit., 606. The popularity of the books by Bellah and his associates is evidence of the concern and eagerness to learn about institutions in our society. The latest book, referred to earlier, *The Good Society*, deals directly with this issue. Also, scholars like Amitai Etzioni are both writing and organizing people to counter the fragmentation in our society. See his *The Spirit of Community: Rights, Responsibilities, and the Communitarian Agenda*(New York: Crown,1993).

[8] Swidler was not referring specifically to theological schools, but rather to the task of recovering the moral foundations of the institutions of our society including the church. In another article in the same publication, Bellah and Adams indicate that our need is not for a new set of institutions so much as the revitalization of our institutions which already have moral meaning: *Ethics and Policy*, Spring 1992; Berkeley: Center for Ethics and Social Policy of the GTU. The Swidler reference is found in a reprint of "The Recession Is Not Just Economic", an editorial in the *Los Angeles Times*, Jan. 8, 1992; the article by Bellah and Adams is entitled "Sources of Hope." "Recovery from our cultural, political and social recession does not mean that we need some new blueprint, some new set of institutions or some new pattern of control...What we truly need is to assure that our institutions have moral meanings, that they support our life together and make a good society possible. This means that we must incorporate life-giving values into the pattern of our lives together, into the institutions that make our relationships with each other possible." 2.

[9] John B. Cobb, Jr.,"Faith seeking understanding: The renewal of Christian thinking," *The Christian Century*, June 29-July 6, 1994 (vol.111), 642.

[10] David Wells, op. cit., 173, though the entire book makes this point.

[11] Dr. Wade Clark Roof of the University of California at Santa Barbara did a sociological study of the views of church leaders regarding presidents of seminaries. While the study did not contain many startling findings, it did reveal that the Lutherans still tend to

regard the presidents of their seminaries more highly than most and are apt to consult with these persons on important issues; this is less true of leaders in other denominations. The smaller, more conservative groups still look to their seminary presidents as charismatic leaders of the denomination.

[12] Robert Wuthnow, *Christianity in the 21st Century: Reflections on the Challenges Ahead* (New York: Oxford University Press, 1993), 50.

[13] Ibid., 16.

[14] Bellah *et al* argue that schools can succeed only if they have a clear mission, and with families and community behind them. While talking about community schools, they reflect on the theological school's need for clarity of mission, with a supporting "family" within the community of the church. *The Good Society*, 176.

[15] Walter Brueggemann,*Texts Under Consideration: The Bible and Postmodern_Imagination* (Minneapolis: Fortress Press,1993), 1-17.

[16] David Ray Griffin, editor, *Spirituality and Society: Postmodern Visions* (Albany: State University of New York Press, 1988).

[17] Douglas Sloan, *Faith and Knowledge: Mainline Protestantism and American Higher Education* (Louisville: Westminster/John Knox Press, 1994). See particularly his final chapter, 212-243.

[18] Kelsey, *To Understand God*, 207.

[19] An interesting parallel is the book by Mark R. Schwehn, *Exiles from Eden: Religion and the Academic Vocation* (New York: Oxford University Press, 1993).

[20] Ibid., vii-viii.

ANNOTATED BIBLIOGRAPHY

In my opinion the first thing a new president or a candidate for the office should do is to read the history of the particular school. I even recommend this for trustees. Nothing takes the place of understanding the school's past, its commitments, and the nuances of its development. I once read fifteen years of the minutes from trustee and faculty meetings of a given institution; believe me, it is revealing.

In addition to that suggestion, I have listed five books which I believe to be very helpful for persons in or considering the office. The books vary in nature and style; some are easy to read and offer practical help; others are more difficult, but provide an excellent underpinning for presidential activity.

Finally, I have selected titles that are of more general interest to presidents, candidates for the position, and trustees whose task is to understand the presidency. While the endnotes provide leads to books dealing with the seminary's purpose and history, the books listed here are to steer interested persons into other areas related to the seminary presidency.

FIVE SIGNIFICANT BOOKS

Kelsey, David H.   *To Understand God Truly: What's Theological About a Theological School.* Louisville: Westminster/John Knox Press, 1992.

I consider this book one of the best studies of theological education in our time. Kelsey analyzes with care the influence of the theological school's tradition, the problems related to stating the institution's purpose, and many of the daily issues of such schools. One does not have to agree with all of his arguments or conclusions to profit greatly from reading the book. The carefully crafted arguments and level of abstraction make reading slow going.

Sloan, Douglas.   *Faith and Knowledge: Mainline Protestantism and American Higher Education.* Louisville: Westminster/ John Knox Press, 1994.

Sloan traces the church's engagement with higher education from the 1950s to the present. As the title suggests, he is concerned about the relation of faith to knowledge. His observations about the possibility of faith in light of contemporary understandings of knowledge illumine much of the struggle which seminaries (and denominations) have experienced.

His concluding chapter points to new possibilities as well as pitfalls. The book deals with both the academy and the church.

Brown, William R.   *Academic Politics.* University, Ala.: The University of Alabama Press, 1982.

This is by far the most helpful explanation of faculty culture; it offers a perspective on the faculty's style of working and the consequences for the management of an institution of higher education. The book illuminates why faculty behave as they do in the political activity of organizing and administering a school. Seminaries and universities are different institutions, but faculty culture is much the same in both.

Birnbaum, Robert.   *How Academic Leadership Works: Understanding Success and Failure in the College Presidency.* San Francisco: Jossey-Bass, 1992.

This volume is one of the fruits of a five-year study of the Institutional Leadership Project directed by Birnbaum at the University of Maryland. It describes what presidents need to do to manage the complex governance arrangements of institutions of higher education. From the perspective of seminary presidents, his neglect of the governing board is unfortunate. It is easy to read, however, and useful.

Bensimon, Estela M.   *Redesigning Collegiate Leadership: Teams and*
Neumann, Anna.   *Teamwork in Higher Education*. Baltimore: The Johns
                        Hopkins University Press, 1993.

This helpful study of the advantages of teamwork in administering an institution of higher education is congenial with with the definition of leadership used in this book. There are helpful guidelines on making teams work as well as warnings about their limitations. The book can be read rapidly and is useful.

OTHER HELPFUL BOOKS

Bellah, Robert   *The Good Society*. New York: Alfred A. Knopf, 1991.
Madsen, Richard
Sullivan, William M.
Swidler, Ann
Tipton, Steven M.

This study is listed because of its helpfulness in understanding institutions and their function in our society. The chapter on education might be of particular interest, especially the notion of revitalizing institutions, not necessarily creating new ones.

Bolman, Lee G.   *Modern Approaches to Understanding and Managing*
Deal, Terrence E.   *Organizations*. San Francisco: Jossey-Bass, 1984.

The rector of a Catholic seminary said this book opened a whole new world of understanding for him. The book is capable of doing this for folk who have little or no understanding of organizations and how one works within them.

Campbell, Thomas C.   *The Gift of Administration*. Philadelphia: The
Reierson, Gary B.   Westminster Press, 1981.

This book reflects theologically on the task of administration as a form of ministry. The focus is on pastors or administrators in churches, but there are insights for theological educators as well.

Chait, Richard Holland, Thomas Taylor, Barbara.	*The Effective Board of Trustees.* New York: Macmillan, 1991.

I suspect this is the single best volume yet to appear on the tasks of trustees and their relationship to the president. How the president "educates" the board is part of the agenda.

Crowley, Joseph N.	*No Equal in the World: An Interpretation of the Academic Presidency* Reno: University of Nevada Press, 1994.

Crowley provides a comprehensive study of the literature on the American academic presidency from the middle of the nineteenth century to the present. There are surveys of critical studies, autobiographies and biographies, and even fictional presidents found in novels. While listing numerous metaphors, descriptions, and required characteristics, the author does not offer any specific interpretation or perspective for our time. It is a useful tool for locating books in one's area of interest.

Drucker, Peter F.	*Managing the Non-Profit Organization.* New York: HarperCollins, 1990.

The writings of Peter Drucker are well known and this volume focuses on institutions that have as their goals the re-shaping of human life, which he argues is the unique feature of not-for-profits.

Fisher, James L.	*Power of the Presidency.* New York: MacMillan, American Council on Education, 1984, *The Board and the President.* New York: MacMillan, American Council on Education, 1991.

Many people disagree with the perspectives of Fisher, but since he states so strongly his point of view, it is worth reading even if you argue with him from time to time.

Holman, Mark Allyn. *Presidential Search in Theological Schools: Process Makes a Difference,*1994. Privately printed as part of the research project on The Study of the Seminary Presidency. Available through the ATS offices.

Holman used the research gathered as part of this project as well as his wide reading to put together these very helpful insights.

Kauffman, Joseph F. *At the Pleasure of the Board: The Service of the College and University President.* Washington, D. C.: American Council on Education.1980.

A classic statement of the relation of president to governing board.

Kelsey, David. *Between Athens and Berlin:The Theological Education Debate.*Grand Rapids: Eerdmans,1993.

I have used Kelsey throughout this book so the reader no doubt has a sense of both his message and style. While his books are not easy to read, they are very important. Here he traces the influence on two major understandings of the academy on theological institutions.

Kerr, Clark, Director. *Presidents Make a Difference: Strengthening Leadership in Colleges and Universities.* Washington, D. C.: Association of Governing Boards, 1984. Kerr and Marian L.Gade.*The Many Lives of Academic Presidents: Time, Place, and Character.* Washington, D. C. : Association of Governing Boards, 1986.

While these books deal with college and university presidents, they have contributed to defining the roles and understanding of the presidency in higher education in the United States in our time.

Nason, John W., assisted by Nancy Axelrod. *Presidential Assessment.* Washington, D. C.: Association of Governing Boards, 1984. *Presidential Search.* Washington, D. C.: Association of Governing Boards, 1980 and 1984.

Both books focus on the presidency in colleges and universities, but are helpful in outlining the issues involved in the evaluation and calling of presidents.

Pacala, Leon.   "The Presidential Experience in Theological
                         Education: A Study of Executive Leadership."
                         Theological Education. vol. xxix, no.1, 11-38.
                         "Reflection on the State of Theological Education
                         in the 1980's" *Theological Education*,vol. xviii,no.1
                         (Autumn 1981), 9-43.

These are earlier studies of the seminary presidency which I have quoted often in this book. Some of the data is out of date, but comparisons are interesting.

Rost, Joseph C.   *Leadership for the Twenty-First Century.* New York:
                         Praeger, 1991.

Of the numerous books available on the subject of leadership, this one does an excellent job of tracing the history of the word, showing the evolution of the various concepts of leadership, and then proposing a definition that is useful in many settings.

Schon, Donald A.   *The Reflective Practitioner:How Professionals Think in
                         Action.* New York: Basic Books, 1983, and *Educating
                         the Reflective Practitioner.* San Francisco: Jossey-Bass,
                         1990.

These books have a distinct usefulness in that they assist presidents in analyzing the relation of thinking and acting, which they are called to do constantly. While he does not settle the theory/practice dilemma that stalks higher education in general, the author is provocative on the subject.

Schuth, Katarina   *Reason for the Hope: the Future of the Roman Catholic
                         Theologates.* Wilmington: Michael Glazier,Inc.,1989.

Schuth has done extensive survey work among Catholic seminaries. She has pulled together very helpful information about the current state of theological institutions and the possible futures.

Senge, Peter M.   *The Fifth Discipline: The Art and Practice of the Learning Organization.* New York: Doubleday/Currency, 1990.

This is one of those books that is capable of prompting a president to reflect on the organizational structure of the school in a fresh way.

Taylor, Barbara E. and Warford, Malcolm L., editors. *Good Stewardship: A Handbook for Seminary Trustees.* Washington,D. C.: Association of Governing Boards of Universities and Colleges, 1991.

This is a helpful collection of essays devoted to aspects of trustee performance and contains individual chapters that can be used for educational events.

Wildavsky, Aaron.   *The Nursing Father: Moses as a Political Leader.* University of Alabama press, 1984.

Wildavsky understands leadership to be determined by the political realities of the context. If one assumes the governance of an educational institution to be the political regime within which one works, this book is interesting and helpful. Obviously Wildavsky's use of Mose and his careful reading of Scripture add to the interest.

Wuthnow, Robert.   *The Restructuring of American Religion: Society and Faith Since World War II.* Princeton: Princeton University Press, 1988. "Pious materialism: How Americans view faith and money." *Christian Century.* Mar.3,1993 (Vol.110,No.7), 238-42.. *Christianity in the Twenty-first Century: Reflections on the Challenges Ahead.* New York: Oxford University Press,1993. *Sharing the Journey: Support Groups and America's New Quest for Community.* New York: The Free Press, 1994.

These books—and he writes them faster than some of us can read them—are very useful as presidents and trustees try to think about tomorrow and the role of the seminary in the life of the church and the world.